How to Build
35 Great Clocks

How to Build
35 Great Clocks

Joseph W. Daniele

Stackpole Books

Published by
STACKPOLE BOOKS
5067 Ritter Road
Mechanicsburg, PA 17055
www.stackpolebooks.com

Printed in the United States of America

Library of Congress Cataloging in Publication Data

Daniele, Joseph William.
How to build 35 great clocks.

Bibliography: p.
1. Clock and watch making.   I. Title.   II. Title: How to build thirty-five great clocks.
TS545.D34   1984   681.1'13   83-24237
ISBN 0-8117-1816-6

ISBN 978-0-8117-2232-2

Contents

SECTION FIVE

Weather Stations

SECTION SIX

Appendix

Acknowledgments

As in all things finite or temporal, I owe a debt of gratitude to many people and organizations for their help in completing this book. Many thanks to the various clock parts suppliers for their pictures and catalogs along with suggestions for possible contents. Several historical museums, such as Colonial Williamsburg and Old Sturbridge Village, as well as the Index of American Design, show many antique clocks from which most of the designs in this book were developed.

Mr. Bert Krasner, a noted photographer, created the cover picture and the individual clock prints. Several woodworking craftsmen added tips and suggestions for actual construction.

To one and all, my warmest thanks for your valuable contributions.

Introduction

Modern hobbyists have discovered clockmaking to be a new outlet for their handiwork. While a clock has always been a beautiful addition to one's home, the gift of a handmade clock often means much more than just a piece of furniture. The clock builder presents a gift rich in pride, skill, thought, and activity. Many "basement workers" have enlarged their hobby activity and now offer their products for sale at flea markets, work fairs, and area antique shows. Many retail consignment-type store outlets are available for craftware made by such part-time workers. Such work and sales can create supplemental income for retired or spare-time woodworkers as well as allow builders to experience the warm, pleasant interaction between buyers and sellers at these local outlets.

A primary aim of this book is to help woodworkers—beginners or experts—design and build period-style clocks, ranging from very simple plaque or single-board clocks to classic early American and Victorian styles, and ending with plans for several full-size tall case clocks.

Little woodworking experience is required to make the reproductions offered in this book. Our instructions have been kept as simple as possible since the intention is to offer quality clock reproductions for as many readers as possible. Therefore, the joinery, assembly, and tool usage have been designed to be understood by everyone, beginner or expert.

In actual construction, the experienced woodworker may wish to add dovetail or spline

In Colonial days, settlers who could not afford private timepieces usually were able to glance up at the church steeple or town hall spire for the time of day. First Church, Longmeadow, Massachusetts.

Spirit of Canterbury Traditional Style Grandfather Tall Case Clock. Kuempel Chime Clockmakers, Excelsior, Minnesota.

Spirit of St. Michael Original Design Tall Case Clock. Kuempel Chime Clockmakers, Excelsior, Minnesota.

Steeple clock. Turncraft Clock Imports Co.,
Golden Valley, Minnesota.

Vienna-type regulator clock. Turncraft Clock Imports Co.,
Golden Valley, Minnesota.

joints, compound miter cuts, or inlaid work into the clock cases. The plans are easily adaptable to such techniques. Since the average hobbyist-woodworker does not always have the machinery, tools, or experience for such complex procedures, our plans were developed to keep operations simple and offer step-by-step techniques for proper construction. They show simple butt or rabbet joinery, and such construction will serve well for all of the clock units. Most often, a certain type of fastener is suggested in the plans, but feel free to make substitutions. Your preference should supersede any text suggestions.

In many cases where moldings are required, three methods are advised: (1) purchase moldings and parts from clock supply outlets; (2) purchase regular stock moldings available from local lumberyards; or (3) create shop-made

moldings with a shaper or a hand-held electric router.

Most of the following plans were designed around a battery-powered, quartz-style movement. The modern quartz movement is a thin, small, factory-sealed movement that is inexpensive and easily installed. For other types of movements, such as key-wound or weight-driven units, the required width and depth measurements should be double-checked; as a rule such movements require more room and space than the battery units. (See drawing of case design for basic measurements.)

It is recommended that the builder have the movement and dial on hand or know the basic measurements before starting construction because sizes and requirements could vary from dealer to dealer. Many dealer catalogs will give movement size measurements, and these can

Vienna-type regulator clock under construction.

be used successfully. (See Appendix for a list of possible suppliers.)

The main purpose of this book is to offer plans for clock reproductions that permit free interpretation by the builder. Because I will not be the same person tomorrow as I was yesterday, if I were to make these same clocks again, I might make them in the same way, or I might change a method or two. Using this book as a starting point for design and sources of available movements, styles, finish, and construction techniques, you, the builder, will make the final statement about how your clock will eventually turn out. The average household clock case offers a rare opportunity to integrate artistic interpretation with purpose. The clock case creates the temple of design in which the goddess of time resides. It is the gathering together of wood, glass, metal, and finish to form a personal family heirloom.

CONSTRUCTION

Modern-day clock construction involves three major choices of components: the movement; the dial, or face; and the housing, or case. A perfect clock is one where the correct balance is achieved among these three. The dial (face and hands) and case are usually of a particular style, often related to a time period. The choice

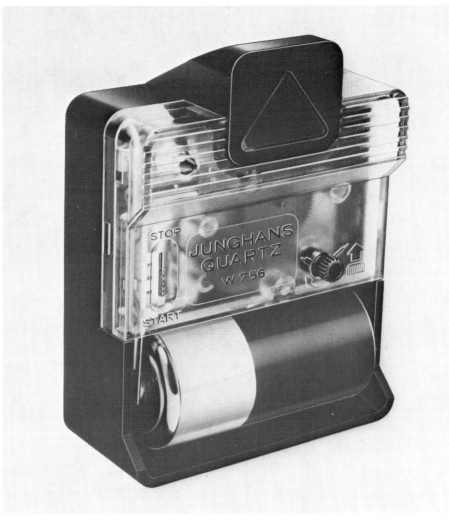

Quartz movement. Time Industries Corporation, Sedalia, Colorado.

of movement depends on the personal preference of the maker. Because an understanding of all of these components is important, certain information will be necessary before starting work.

MOVEMENTS

The movement is the mechanism that keeps the precise time and moves the hands around the dial (time ring) in accurate measured units. The power to turn the hands in precise measured beats comes from one of several different sources: battery, household electric current, key-wound spring, or weight drive.

Some complex clock movements are designed to perform functions other than keeping accurate rates of time; they depict seconds, drive a pendulum, announce the hour or half hour, play a melody on the hour, show phases of the moon, or keep track of months and years. The more functions involved, the larger the movement and power required. The cost of the movement can range from under ten dollars for modern battery-quartz movements to over several thousand dollars for some weight-driven, twelve-tube musical movements.

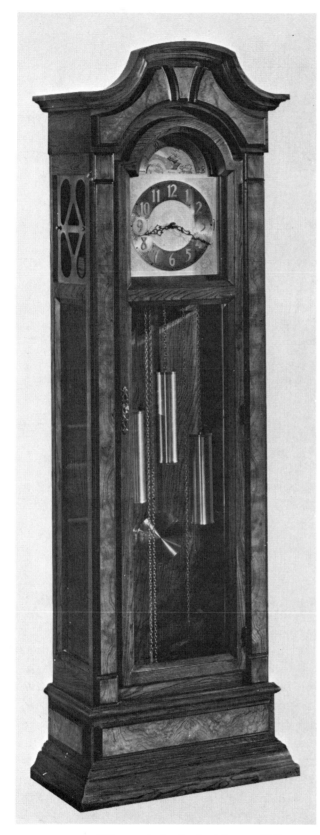

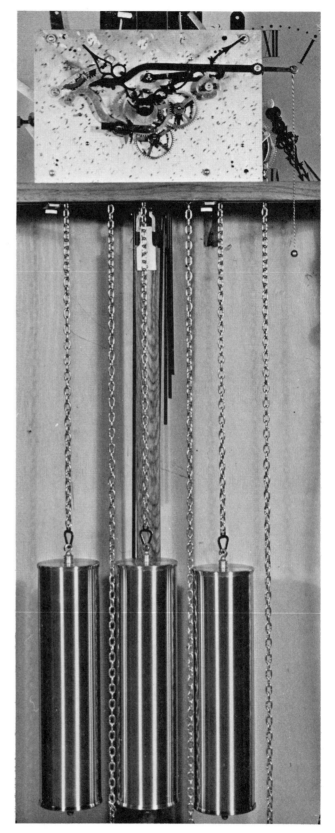

Tall case clock, classic-style grandfather case. Heritage Clock Co., Lexington, North Carolina.

Weight-driven tall case movement. Mason and Sullivan, West Yarmouth, Massachusetts.

Movements vary in size from less than 1" to over 9" deep, depending upon the functions they must perform and the method of drive employed.

For the purpose of this book, most of the clocks were designed around modern battery-powered quartz movements. Notes are given, where applicable, for alternate design if additional depth is needed for key or weight movements.

The *key wind* is a movement in which the wound-up spring provides power for the clock drive and any bell or tone. Such springs must be wound every one to thirty days. Access most often is through an open door, with key access in the clockface. The uncoiling power of the spring is controlled by the clock's escapement function.

Weight-driven clocks depend upon a weight on a chain or cable over a sprocket. The downward pull of the weights powers the movement and strikes the hour by means of controlled escapements. The weights must be pulled back up to a starting position as the clock winds down. Access most often is available through a door opening under the movement seat.

The normal *electric-drive* unit is one that plugs into the household electric outlet. This is a "set it, forget it" operation, and unless electric power is interrupted, the clock keeps perfect time and runs unattended for many years.

Battery-operated movements have several advantages. They will run from one to three years on a single alkaline battery. The clock can be placed anywhere, and the new quartz units are very accurate. Access for battery replacement most often is through a small rear opening or removal of the clock face.

Movement Second Hands

Most electrical-power and some mechanical-power movements have second hands. The second hand can be one of two varieties: the sweep (continuous movement) or the step (stop

Weight-driven movement.
Mason and Sullivan, West Yarmouth, Massachusetts.

and go). Most often the second hand fits outside the hour and minute hands and works via a small fitting inside the movement shaft.

Adjustment and Controls

In the mechanical movement hand, adjustments are made by pushing the actual minute or hour hands forward or backward. Since the hour hand is a pressure fit, it can be placed to point anywhere on the clock dial. However, if an hour tone strike is employed, the position of the hour hand must coincide with the num-

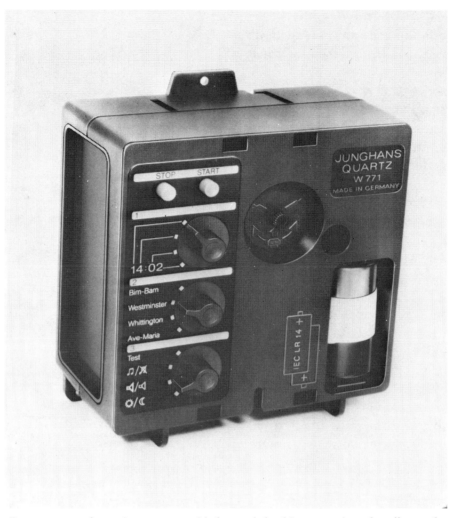

Battery-quartz electronic movement with four-melody chime operation, shutoff control, and volume control.
Time Industries Corporation, Sedalia, Colorado.

ber of tones or strikes. The movement of the minute hand conducts the whole operation, moving the hour pointer in conjunction with the strike counter, moon dials, and so on.

The electrical control or setting-adjustment knobs are either on the back or side of the units. When a case is constructed, access must be allowed so that the hands can be set when needed. Most movement catalogs state whether movements are rear- or side-adjusted.

A few clocks have a calendar sweep hand, or separate date indicator, working off the movement. The larger hall or tall case clocks, and some mantel clocks, have moon-phase dials controlled by the time movement. Directions

for fitting and setting are included in the manufacturer's instructions.

Pendulums fall into two major categories: those required for timekeeping (an escapement unit), and those nonfunctional models installed for effect. In many mechanical-driven movements, the pendulum swing controls the escapement, or "ticktock," accuracy for the timepiece. Faster or slower adjustments are made by moving the pendulum bob up or down the pendulum rod. Such a pendulum clock movement requires a perfectly level setting to keep correct time and keep running.

The nonfunctioning battery-operated pendulum works independently of the clock timekeeping action. In fact, the pendulum could be stopped, or even taken away, and it would not affect the timekeeping accuracy of the movement. Battery movements are available where the pendulum produces the sought-after ticktock sound. Very often one battery powers the clock while another battery powers the independent pendulum.

While working with pendulum movements, the important factors are the rod or pendulum length and the side-to-side arc or movement. Most often the length ranges from 4"–30", and is measured from the center hand shaft to the bottom of the pendulum bob. The side movement, or swing, is measured in overall arc or distance from each side of a plumb center. Example: a 6" swing would be 3" each side of dead center. The clock case must be large enough to accept this swing. It is recommended that an extra inch or more on each side of the swing be allowed. In the example of a 6" pendulum swing, an inside case width of 8" is recommended.

There are scores of different styles and sizes of clock hands. Some are the huge, bold modern styles, while others are metal with intricate scrollwork and are appropriate for use in Colonial or early American models.

A full set of clock hands could include the hour and minute hands, a sweep second hand,

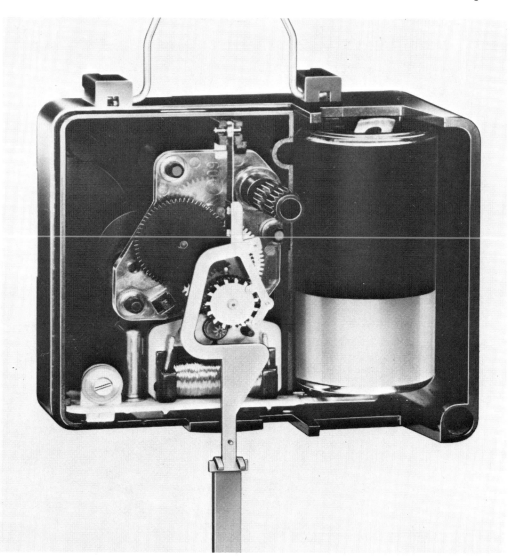

Battery-operated quartz movement with pendulum. Time Industries Corporation, Sedalia, Colorado.

23

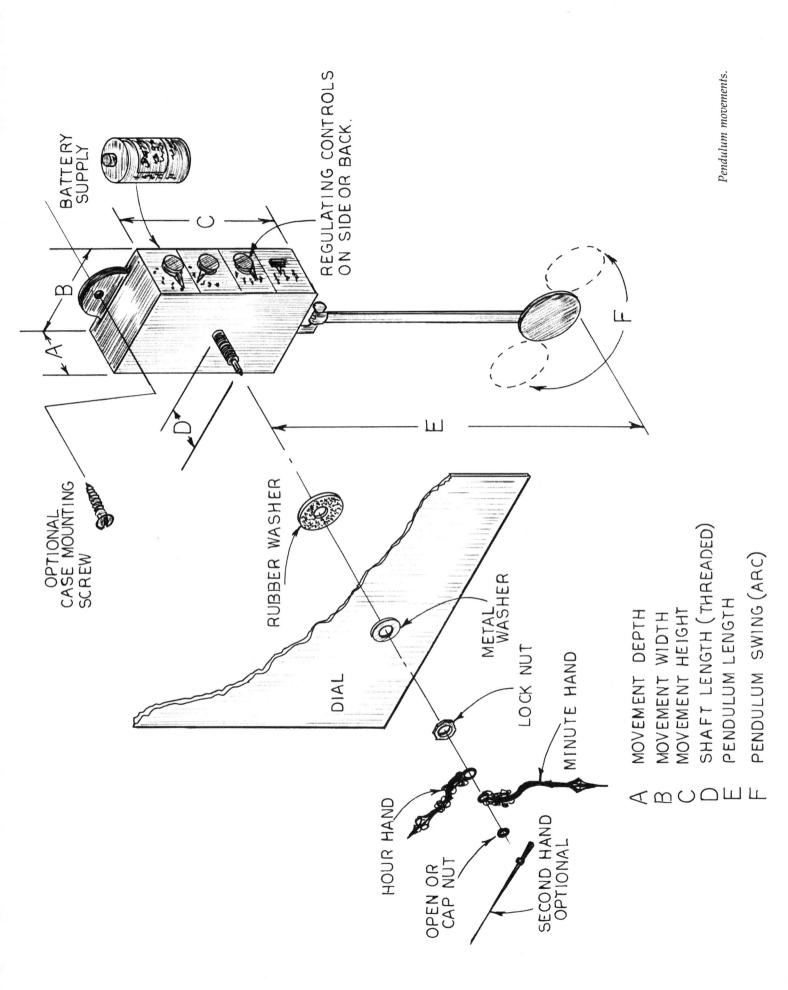

BATTERY SUPPLY

REGULATING CONTROLS ON SIDE OR BACK.

OPTIONAL CASE MOUNTING SCREW

RUBBER WASHER

DIAL

METAL WASHER

LOCK NUT

MINUTE HAND

OPEN OR CAP NUT

HOUR HAND

SECOND HAND OPTIONAL

A   MOVEMENT DEPTH
B   MOVEMENT WIDTH
C   MOVEMENT HEIGHT
D   SHAFT LENGTH (THREADED)
E   PENDULUM LENGTH
F   PENDULUM SWING (ARC)

Pendulum movements.

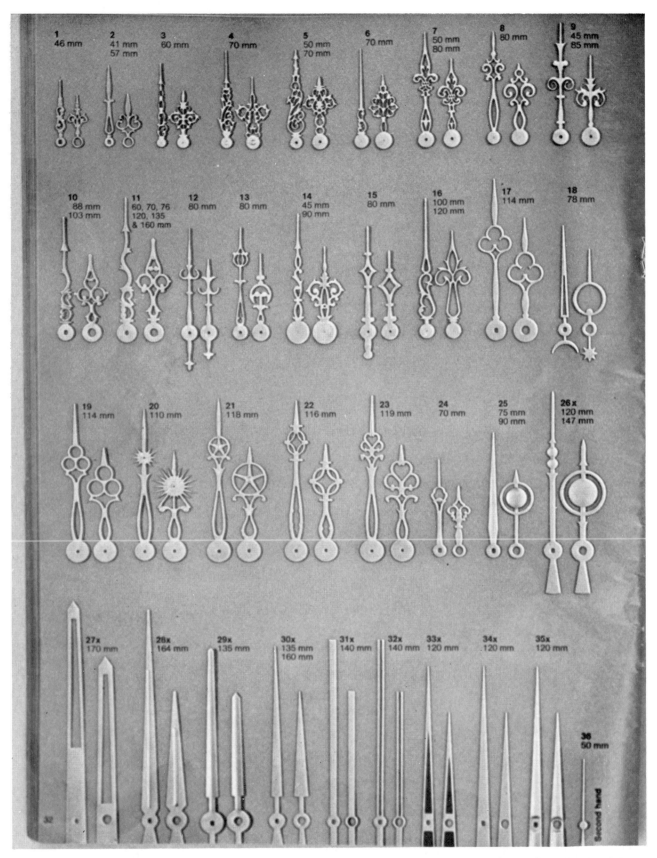

Sample clock hands. Otto Frei—Jules Borel, Oakland, California.

25

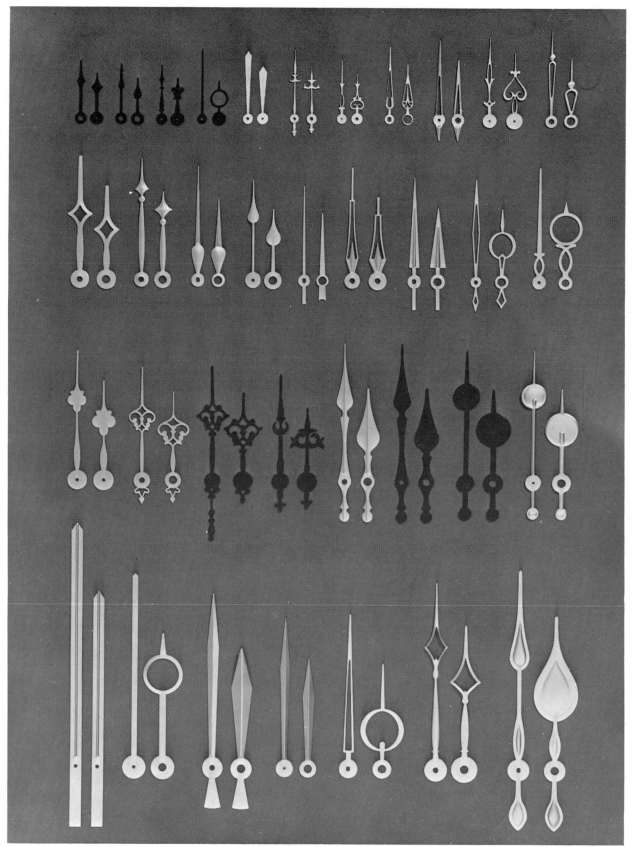

Assorted clock hands. Selva Borel Company, Oakland, California.

26

and a calendar hand or pointer.

In making clocks, design compatibility of the hand and dials should be sought. Check antique pieces, catalog pictures, or museums for possible combinations. Most suppliers recommend certain style hands for certain movements. You will soon develop an eye for the right combination to achieve a matching of all units.

For most clock movements, the hour hand is a pressure fit on the movement shaft. This means that the hour hand is pushed onto the shaft and friction holds it in place. When installing the hour hand, push it onto the movement shaft with pressure near the shaft, so as not to bend the very delicate metal. If the fit is loose, the handhole flange can be crimped with pliers in order to achieve a tighter fit.

The minute hand has an oblong straight-sided hole that fits on a threaded matched stud in the movement shaft. The minute hand is held in place by a locking nut. This nut can be open (hole in center) or closed. If a sweep second hand is to be installed, however, an open nut must be used. Second hands are driven by a very small pin which is found inside the center of the movement shaft. The second hand is also a pressure fit.

Installing Movement Hands

1. Install the minute hand in place temporarily. By means of the rear time-adjustment knob, turn the minute hand until it points to 12 o'clock. Remove the minute hand.

2. Push the hour hand onto the movement shaft, pointing toward a selected hour. If the hour hand is too loose, crimp the center flange very lightly with pliers.

3. After the hour hand is in place, install the minute hand with the locking nut. Finger pressure on the nut should be enough to keep it tight.

4. Install the second hand if one is used.

5. Turn the movement-hand control knob at the rear of the movement, and watch the hands cross over each other as they rotate around the dial. Make sure the hands do not touch each other. The hour or minute hand can be slightly bent to achieve clearance. Check to see that the hour hand does not touch the clock face as it rotates around. If a glass cover (bezel) is used, check to see that the hands do not come in contact with the glass at any point. Hands touching each other, the dial, or the glass cover slow down the movement and disrupt its accuracy.

6. If a "bim-bam," or accumulative hour strike, tone is used, the appropriate hour and number of tones will have to be synchronized. Each movement may employ a different method to accomplish hour, minute, and tone synchronization. Follow the manufacturer's recommendations carefully.

Dial (Face)

One retail clock catalog boasts that it contains over two hundred different dials. This wide assortment is the general rule, and not the exception, for most suppliers. Clock dials are made in many shapes, sizes, styles, and motifs. Numerically, there are two styles: Roman numerals and Arabic digits. Some modern clock dials have no digits at all—only dots, dashes, stars, or zodiac signs; other clock styles call for only the 3-, 6-, 9-, and 12-digit series, sometimes with markers in between.

Stick-on, self-adhesive-back dots, dashes, or numerals are available for the clockmaker who may want to make his own dial. With these different components, anything and everything can therefore be turned into a dial. A typical example of this type of self-contained construction would be a free-form slab of wood, with the stick-on dots, and a numeral and quartz movement recessed into the plank back.

Purchased stock dials may be made of metal, plastic, or paper. They are round, square, rectangular, or topped with a peaked or rounded top. They may be painted with scenes or cov-

Sample clock dials; features round, square, and time ring dials. Otto Frei—Jules Borel, Oakland, California.

ered with delicate floral and scroll designs. Some, such as those used for most Shaker clocks, are very plain. To compound the dial inventory still further, dials come in several different sizes.

Basically, each clock dial, regardless of design, represents a full circle of some sort involving 360 degrees divided into equal sections. Often the dial is divided into five-minute intervals, numbered from 1 to 12, to represent minutes and hours.

The placement of numerals is called the "time ring." Some dials may have several time rings —one for the hour numerals, another inside or

Assorted clock dials. Selva Borel Company, Oakland, California.

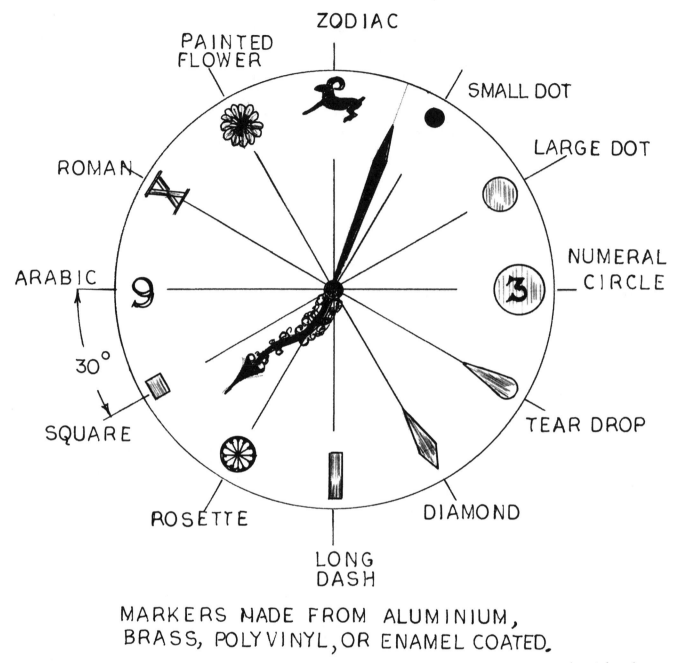

ZODIAC

PAINTED
FLOWER

SMALL DOT

LARGE DOT

ROMAN

NUMERAL
CIRCLE

ARABIC

30°

SQUARE

TEAR DROP

ROSETTE

DIAMOND

LONG
DASH

MARKERS MADE FROM ALUMINIUM,
BRASS, POLYVINYL, OR ENAMEL COATED.

Assorted markers.

outside to show the minutes—and some may even have a calendar date ring, numbered 1 to 31.

The dial is usually protected by a glass door or covering. A self-contained unit consisting of a round metal frame, glass, dial, and hardware is called a bezel. This bezel is designed with a convex pane of glass held in a metal ring hinged to another ring surrounding a fixed dial. Manufacturers offer many different sizes and styles of bezels.

If the clock does not have its own glass bezel-type door, the plans will call for a shop-made door, to be opened for time setting, key winding, or weight movements. The glass for such doors may be obtained with beveled edges and painted scenes, silk-screened with stripes or rear images. Plain window or nonreflective glass may be purchased from glass or hardware outlets.

If the glass is to be purchased from one of the various clock suppliers, then the case should be designed to accommodate the glass. Do not make the case first, hoping to purchase the correct size beveled glass from a supply outlet. It would be wise to have the glass on hand before starting construction.

Many mail-order and retail clock outlets sell kits to make different styles of clock units. These kits may include the wood (precut), molding, plans, movement, dial, and glass. The price is related to the amount of material and labor involved in the total kit. Because the precut kit wood is designed for one type and size of clock, no interpretation, alteration, or personal styling is allowed for. The kit makes the clock in the kit plan, and very little else.

The same kit outlets sell wood parts in several different species. These parts are the difficult wood fittings, too complicated for the average person to make in a home workshop. Such premade parts include lathe-turned columns, finials, scrolls, swan-necks, rosettes, and moldings. Brass fittings, hardware, and metal scrolls are also available. These premade parts are very helpful when one lacks sophisticated tools.

When the dial, movement, and hands are ordered, the necessary wood parts can also be included.

The clock reproductions offered in this book are designed, with few exceptions, to be made with available materials and common hand

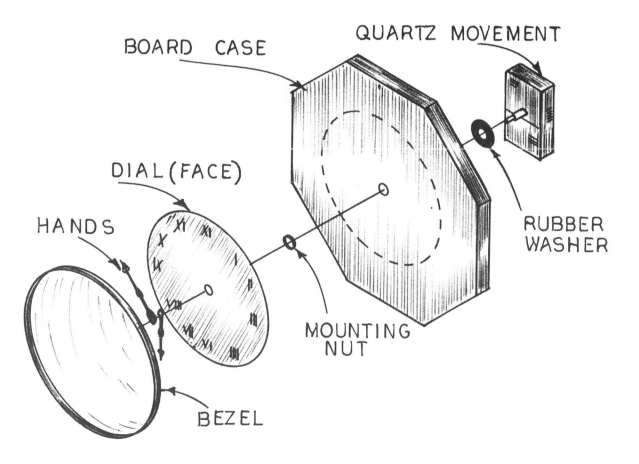

Sample bezel/dial.

Assorted finials. Selva Borel Company, Oakland, California.

tools, including hand-held electric tools found in the average basement workshop. A saber saw, router, and orbital sander are the only suggested power tools, but many clock models can be made with only a miter box and hand tools. Material may be purchased from any retail building supply or hobby outlet. If moldings are suggested in the construction, the selection has been made from millwork available in any lumberyard, or from shop-made routed moldings.

All of the offered reproductions have been developed from historical pieces very often found in museums or restoration settlements, such as Old Sturbridge Village. Each offering contains a material list with suggested woods. Feel free, however, to make changes or substi-

tutions. Along with a material list, the text suggests one or more movements, dial and hand size, and style.

Once again, it is strongly recommended that the builder have the clock parts on hand before starting work because of possible variations in movement sizes and placement. Offered in the Appendix is a supplier list that will help you obtain clock supplies and catalogs. I have purchased materials from most of these suppliers and have found them to be honest, punctual, and reliable. However, this is not an unqualified recommendation of only these particular suppliers; I am sure there are other outlets that are just as reliable. To save time and postage, you may wish to check local hobby or retail outlets before ordering by mail.

MOVEMENT MEASUREMENTS

Any clock case must be designed with certain measurements in mind. The wood case must be large enough to accept the movement depth, width, and height. The size of the case can vary greatly depending upon the movement used. A battery-quartz movement requires much less interior room than weight-driven models do, and some battery movements are extra thin in order to be contained within a single ¾" board thickness.

The hand shaft length can also vary greatly. Some units are extra long for thick wooden dials, or extra short for thin metal dials. Atten-tion should be paid to these details when ordering supplies from mail-order outlets, or when purchasing over the counter.

Two possible methods may be used to fasten the movement to the wood case. The first method is to secure the movement to the case itself with built-up blocks and screws. With the movement centered and secured, the dial is installed over the movement shaft arm and held there with a washer and threaded nut. The second method is to fasten the movement to the clock dial itself, by means of a washer and locknut on the threaded movement shaft arm. The "dial movement" assembly is then secured to the clock case, with screws (or pins), through the dial itself into a frame or set of dial cleats. The dial frame or cleats can be a solid wood

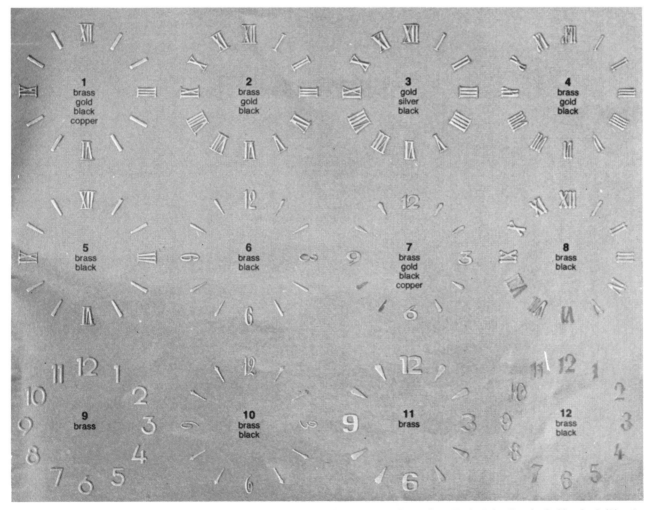

Assorted time ring markers. Otto Frei—Jules Borel, Oakland, California.

33

Moving moon dial; type used in grandfather, grandmother, and some carriage-style clocks. Mason and Sullivan, West Yarmouth, Massachusetts.

backer board, or a frame made of 1½″-wide stock screwed or nailed into the interior of the clock case. (See case design drawing.)

Most often the actual size of the dial frame or cleats is determined by the width used for the door rail and stiles.

SECURING THE UNITS

Most often when a door (doorframe) is used, the clockface (dial) will be the same size as the glass panel area within the doorframe. Thus,

if a 7⅞″ or 200mm square or round face is used, most often the door will be designed so that the glass area will be at least 8″. This will allow the whole face to be exposed to view. However, the typical doorframe members may be 1¼″ or 1½″ wide, and the case body will have an exterior sidewall thickness of ¾″. This could create a ½″–¾″ space between the clockface and surrounding case sides. A dial frame or cleat fills in this void and creates a means to secure the face in place.

As an example, if a typical clock case uses an 8″ dial, with a glass door made up of 1½″-wide rail/stile members, the exterior clock case width

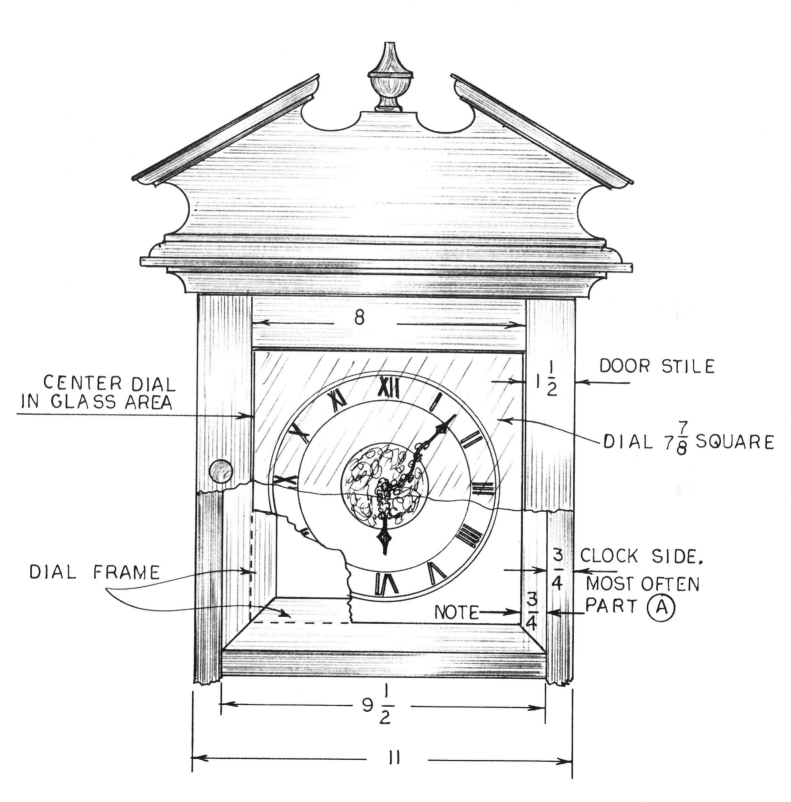

CENTER DIAL
IN GLASS AREA

DOOR STILE

$1\frac{1}{2}$

DIAL $7\frac{7}{8}$ SQUARE

8

DIAL FRAME

$\frac{3}{4}$ CLOCK SIDE,
MOST OFTEN
PART Ⓐ

NOTE $\frac{3}{4}$

$9\frac{1}{2}$

11

Case design.

35

will be 8″ + 1½″ + 1½″ for a total of 11″. If the clock side pieces (most often Part A) are ¾″ thick, the result will be an interior case width of 9½″ used to contain a dial of 8″, or a space 1½″ larger than the dial itself. The dial frame, cleat, or backer board will fill in this area, and this provides the means to secure the dial in place in the center of the glass door panel.

Access

Allowance should be made for access to the movement power source, time- or hand-adjustment lever, and any other settings required.

Most often these units are located at the back of the movement.

Very often the back of the clock case is cut out, or a small door is installed to allow for battery replacement. Many times I have found the clock case too beautiful to cut holes into; I have elected to change batteries or make any necessary adjustment by way of removing the installed clock dial and gaining access to the movement from the front. Since the quartz movement will operate for at least a year on one battery, replacement is an infrequent problem. The builder may decide which replacement method is preferable. No special note is made of replacement access in the following plans.

SECTION ONE

Simple Wall,
or Plaque-style, Clocks

Slate dial, painted. Ms. Sharon Kida, Chester, Massachusetts.

Tin, pewter, or china dishes make excellent dials when used with self-contained designs depicting the hours, such as an arrangement of flowers or similar designs around a time ring. Self-sticking numerals, dots, dashes, or animated symbols may be used if preferred.

China dishes present a small problem in that a center hole for the movement hand shaft must be drilled. This problem can be overcome by having a local glass cutter, tiler, or glazier drill the hole for you at a nominal fee.

MAKING A SINGLE-BOARD, OR PLAQUE, CLOCK

1. Lay out the desired shape full size on paper. With a compass, draw a circle for the dial area, time ring, or bezel frame. Check clock catalogs for available sizes, shapes, designs, and numeral series. The paper pattern will allow viewing the proposed clock/board/dial relationship before cutting the actual wood.

2. Transfer the pattern to the selected wood

stock. Cut out the wood design. If a molded edge is to be used, create one with a hand-held router and bit, and route out the desired design. Sand the edges smooth.

3. Mark the size of the clock movement in the center of the plaque. With a drill and chisel (or router, if available), cut out the required recess for the movement in the board back. Drill a ½" diameter hole through the board center for the movement hand shaft. If a full dial or bezel unit is to be used, a through recess hole can be cut into the board because the dial or bezel will cover the area.

4. In mounting a full dial or bezel, the movement can be attached to the dial by means of a threaded nut on the threaded hand shaft. When the dial or bezel is attached to the board, the unit will be self-contained. In mounting a time ring or individual stick-on members, the movement is inserted into the plaque recess and held secure with a washer and nut on the threaded hand shaft. With the works secured, the time ring or markers are arranged around the center shaft in equal divisions.

UNIQUE, OR ONE-OF-A-KIND, CLOCKS

Some excellent clocks have been made by using household items for the face, or dial.

Needlepoint and hooked or embroidered samplers secured to a wood frame make beautiful and unique clocks. They not only tell time

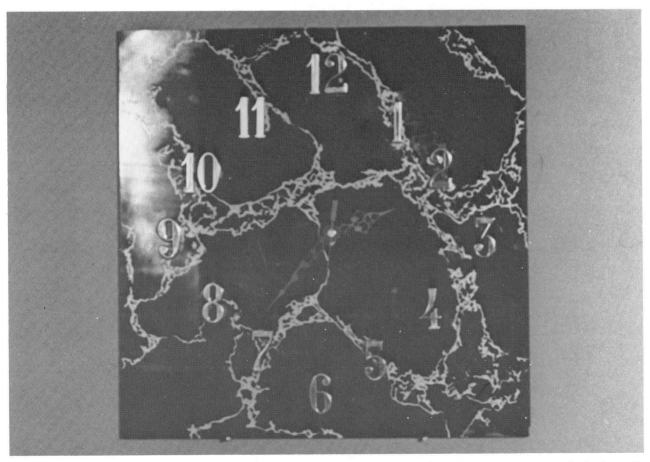

Dial made from a 12" x 12" standard mirror tile.

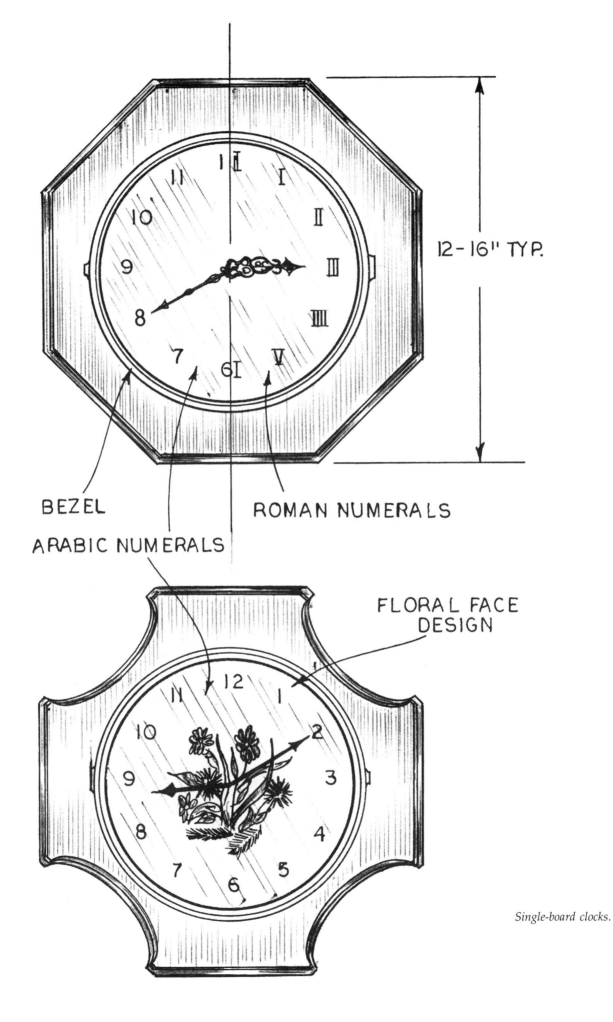

12 – 16" TYP.

BEZEL

ARABIC NUMERALS

ROMAN NUMERALS

FLORAL FACE
DESIGN

Single-board clocks.

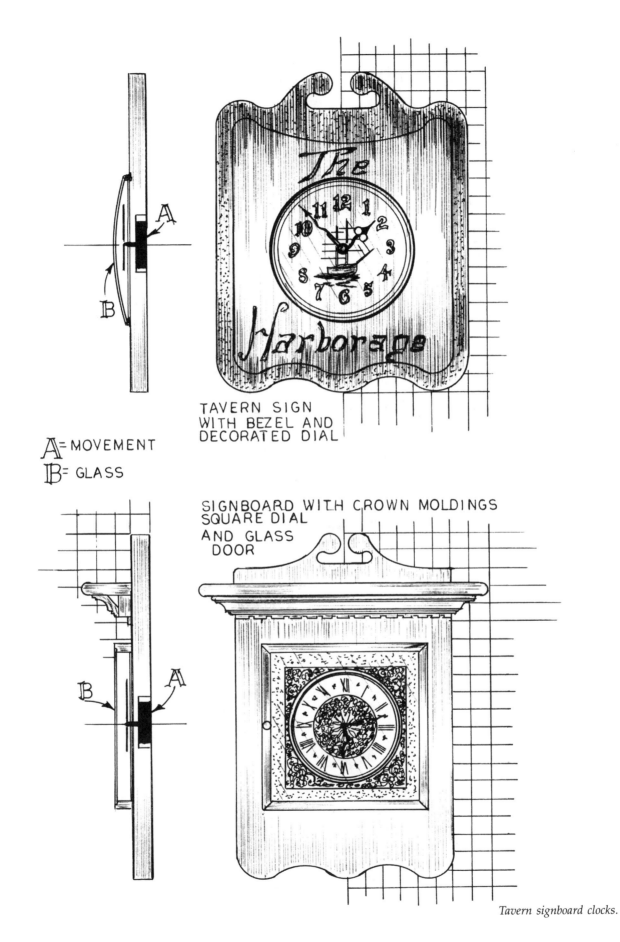

TAVERN SIGN
WITH BEZEL AND
DECORATED DIAL

A= MOVEMENT
B= GLASS

SIGNBOARD WITH CROWN MOLDINGS
SQUARE DIAL
AND GLASS
DOOR

Tavern signboard clocks.

SINGLE BOARD CLOCKS

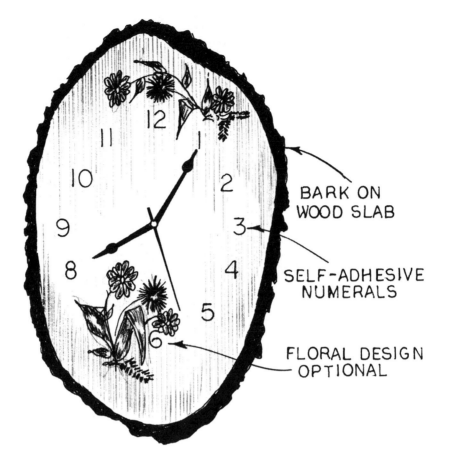

BARK ON
WOOD SLAB

SELF-ADHESIVE
NUMERALS

FLORAL DESIGN
OPTIONAL

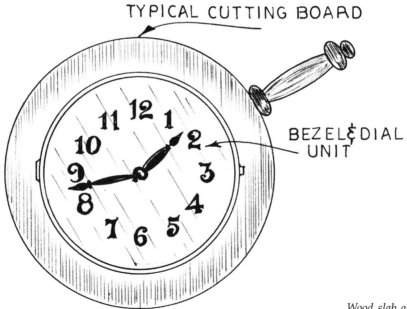

TYPICAL CUTTING BOARD

BEZEL & DIAL
UNIT

Wood slab and cutting board clocks.

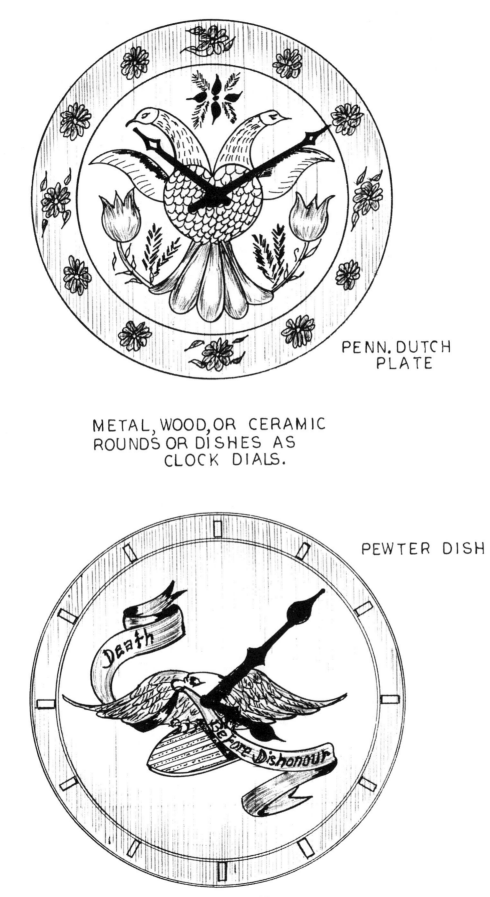

PENN. DUTCH
PLATE

METAL, WOOD, OR CERAMIC
ROUNDS OR DISHES AS
CLOCK DIALS.

PEWTER DISH

Dish clock dials.

43

Slate with time ring. Clock made by Sharon Kida, Chester, Massachusetts.

but display the handiwork of the hobbyist.

Children's toys, such as play building blocks glued together, can be made into a nursery or child's room clock. A unique kitchen clock can be made from a tray, cooking pan, cutting board, cookie form or sheet, or pierced pie-tin panels. Since quartz movements can be purchased with different hand shaft lengths, they are adaptable to almost any material used for the clock dial. Some vendors sell clock movements that will run backward (counterclockwise) to produce a rather unusual result!

44

Black Forest-style Wall Clock

The following clock concept was developed from several different wall-type clocks that go under a general heading called "Black Forest Wall Clocks." The actual clock is centered around a large decorative backboard that often resembles a "grandfather"-style face. Many times a highly decorative pendulum and odd-shaped weights are used in order to enhance the total design.

Material List

Part	Number	Size	Material
A Sides	2	3½" x 9" x ¾"	Pine
B Top	1	3½" x 6½" x ¾"	
C Back	1	7¼" x 8½" x ¼"	Plywood
D Face	1	12" x 16½" x ¾"	
E Dowel Keys	4	⅜" dia. x 2"	

This simple clock can be made using only hand tools. A router and bit are suggested but are optional.

CONSTRUCTION

1. Lay out and cut Parts A, B, and C to suggested shape and size. Plain butt joints can be used to join Part A to Part B. A rabbet should be cut into the rear inside edges of Parts A and B. Part C is nailed into these rabbets.

2. Lay out and cut Part D to suggested shape. Center Part D over the premade box assembly made by Parts A, B, and C. Mark out the back of Part D for the ⅜" diameter dowel keys, Parts E. Mark the edges of Parts A for the dowel keys. Drill the required ⅜" diameter holes into Part D and the edges of Parts A. The drill depth in Part D is ½", while the drill depth into Parts A should be 1¾". The dowel keys, Parts E, are glued into Part D only, making tenons that fit the dowel key hole mortises in Parts A.

Black Forest-style wall clock.

45

REPEAT PATTERN
ON OTHER CORNER

Full-size rose pattern.

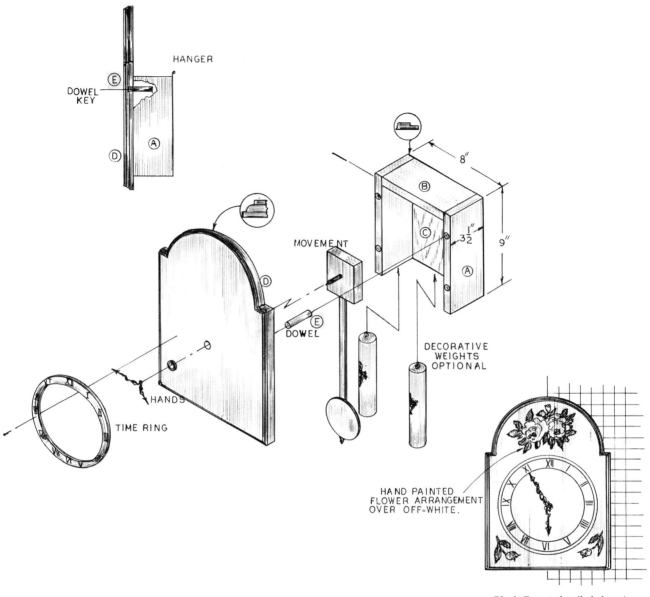

HANGER

DOWEL KEY

E

D · A

MOVEMENT

B

8"

C

3½"

9"

A

D

E
DOWEL

DECORATIVE
WEIGHTS
OPTIONAL

HANDS

TIME RING

HAND PAINTED
FLOWER ARRANGEMENT
OVER OFF=WHITE.

Black-Forest detailed drawing.

3. Finish: Set and fill all nailheads. Sand the entire clock case smooth. Paint with several coats of selected finish. A pure white or off-white color may be used if desired. After the selected finish has dried, hand-paint a flower design on the face. (See drawings for suggestions.) A rose flower pattern is suggested for the face crown; however, any pattern may be used, and such designs may be obtained from greeting cards, magazines, or pattern books. After the design work is completed, coat the clock face with a protective covering such as lacquer or varnish.

4. Drill a mounting hole in the clockface center. Mount a selected movement to the face using washers and a shaft nut. Mount a time ring on the clockface and the desired hands on the movement shaft. Decorative weights may be used, and these are available from the clock movement suppliers. Install a wall hanger ring to the center of Part B and mount the clock on a selected wall.

Wall Clock

Wag-on-the-wall clock.
Turncraft Clock Imports Co., Golden Valley, Minnesota.

This simple wall-wag, plaque-type clock can be made with a simple box base and decorative front plaque.

Material List

Part	Number	Size
A Sides	4	2½″ x 7″ (or 9″) x ¾″
B Back	1	7½″ x 9½″ x ¼″
C Front	1	14″ x 16″ x ¾″

Bezel and dial combination
Quartz movement with pendulum

CONSTRUCTION

1. Lay out and cut the four sides to size. Cut a ¼″ x ¼″ rabbet on the rear inside edges of all four pieces. Nail the four pieces together to form a box. Nail the back, Part B, into the premade rabbets.

2. Lay out and cut the front plaque. The front may be attached to the box with dowels or screws. Lay out and mark the bezel unit to the front plaque. A movement hole will be required in the plaque center.

3. Set and fill all nail holes. Sand the entire clock case smooth. Cover all screwheads with plugs or buttons. Stain or paint the case to a color of choice. Cover with several coats of lacquer or similar finish. Finish with a coat of paste wax. Install the dial/bezel/movement to the front plaque with screws or nails. Install a hanger bracket.

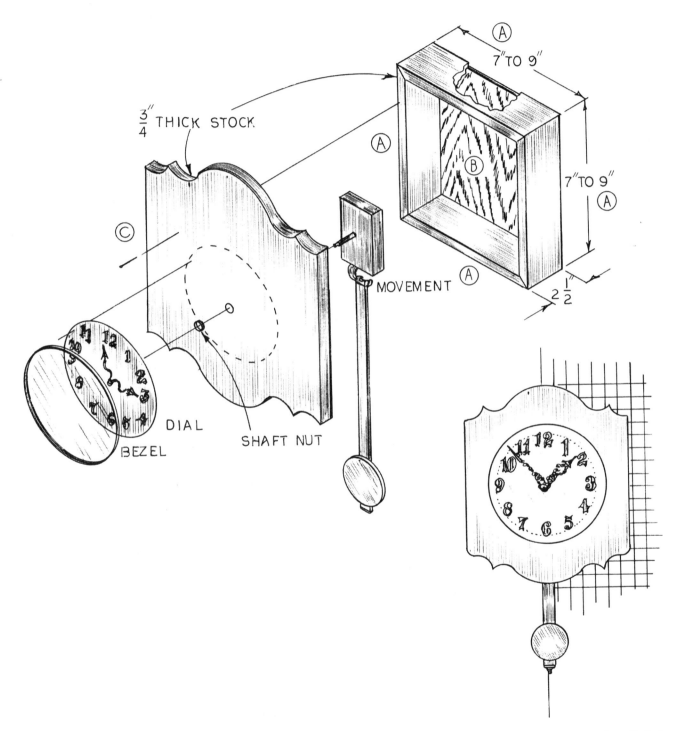

$\frac{3}{4}''$ THICK STOCK

(A) 7" TO 9"

(A)

(A) 7" TO 9"

(B)

(A)

(C)

MOVEMENT

(A)

$2\frac{1}{2}''$

DIAL

SHAFT NUT

BEZEL

Simple wall clock.

49

Eagle Wag-on-the-Wall Clock

Many early clockmakers carved motifs into their cases. The American eagle became a favorite during and after the Revolutionary War. The following clock is a combination of the carved eagle and wag-on-the-wall case.

Material List

Part	Number	Size
A Front	1	15″ x 18″ x ¾″
B Sides	2	2½″ x 14″ x ¾″
C Top	1	2½″ x 10″ x ¾″
D Bottom	1	2½″ x 10″ x ¾″

10″ or 12″ bezel and dial combination
Movement of choice with 8″–10″ pendulum

CONSTRUCTION

1. Lay out and cut the front, sides, top, and bottom pieces, Parts A, B, C, and D. In the bottom piece, Part D, cut a slot to allow the movement pendulum to swing freely. Nail the sides, Parts B, into the top and bottom pieces, Parts C and D.

2. Lay out the shield-shaped front, Part A. Trace on the selected design. Carve or burn the eagle design into the face board. Cut a movement seat, or relief hole, in the center of Part A. Nail or screw the front to the box assembly. *Note: The box can have a back piece if preferred. This back piece should have an access opening for battery replacement or movement adjustments.*

3. Set and fill all nailheads. Cover all screwheads with plugs. Sand entire case smooth. Stain or paint to a color of choice. (See Appendix for suggestions.) Cover with several coats of lacquer or similar finish. Finish with paste wax.

4. Secure the clock movement to the selected bezel. (Most often this is completed with a nut and washer.) Mount the bezel to the front shield piece. Attach a wall hanger bracket.

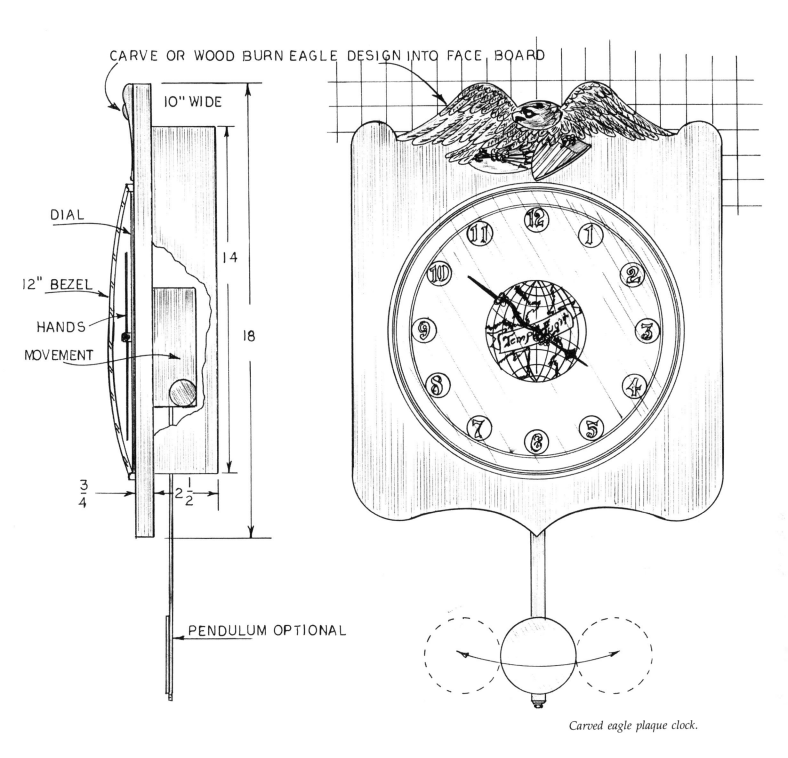

CARVE OR WOOD BURN EAGLE DESIGN INTO FACE BOARD

10" WIDE

DIAL

12" BEZEL

HANDS

MOVEMENT

14

18

$\frac{3}{4}$

$2\frac{1}{2}$

PENDULUM OPTIONAL

Carved eagle plaque clock.

51

Carved Wall Wag

Painted, carved wall clock.

The following clock is a composite of several early American pieces that employed a carved shell design. This case was painted and antiqued using the procedure outlined in the Appendix under *Finishing*.

Material List

Part	Number	Size
A Sides	2	3½" x 16" x ¾"
B Back	1	8" x 18" x ⅜"
C Top	1	3½" x 8¾" x ¾"
D Front	1	11" x 14" x ¾"

8"–9" dia. bezel and dial
Movement of choice with 6"–10" pendulum

CONSTRUCTION

1. Lay out and cut Parts A, B, and C to shape and size. (See full-size patterns for designs.) Cut a ⅜" x ⅜" rabbet on the rear inside edges of Parts A. Cut a ⅜" x ¾" rabbet into both ends of Part C. Nail Part C into Parts A. Nail Part B into the rabbets in Parts A.

2. Lay out and cut Part D to shape and size. (See full-size pattern.) Carve the shell design into the top of Part D. Mark the bezel location, and cut a seat or relief hole for the clock movement in the front piece. An access hole can be cut into Part B for battery replacement if desired. Screw Part D to Parts A and C. Cover the screwheads with plugs or buttons.

3. Set and fill all nailheads. Sand project smooth. Stain or paint to a color of choice. (See Appendix under *Finishing* for suggestions.) Attach the clock movement to the selected dial/bezel. Secure the bezel to the clock case front, Part D.

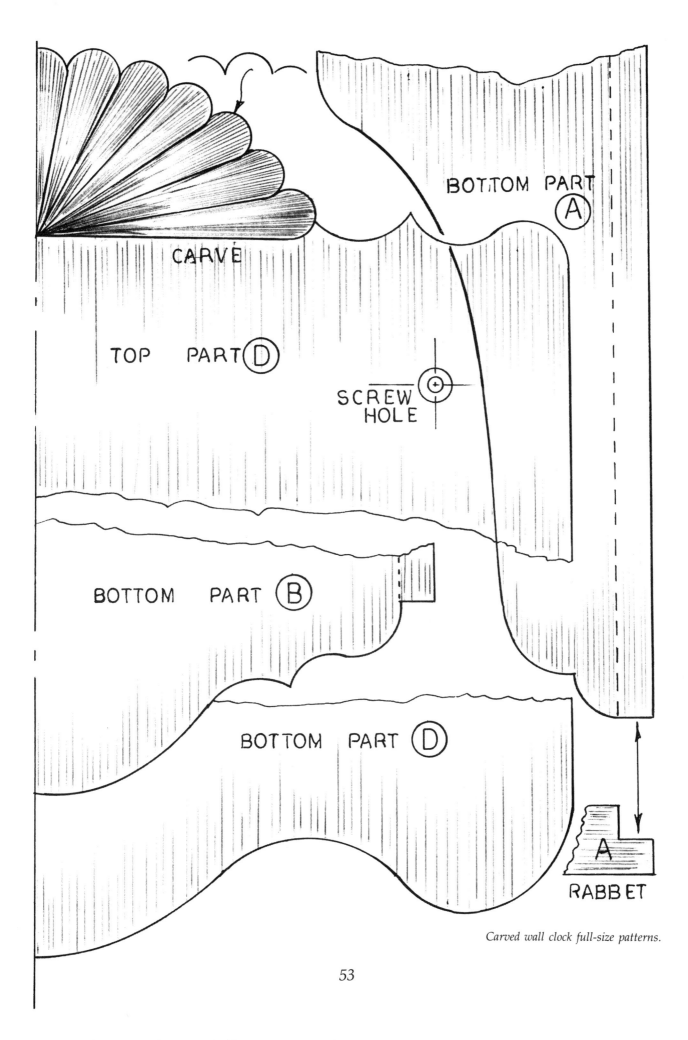

CARVE

BOTTOM PART Ⓐ

TOP PART Ⓓ

SCREW HOLE

BOTTOM PART Ⓑ

BOTTOM PART Ⓓ

Ⓐ

RABBET

Carved wall clock full-size patterns.

53

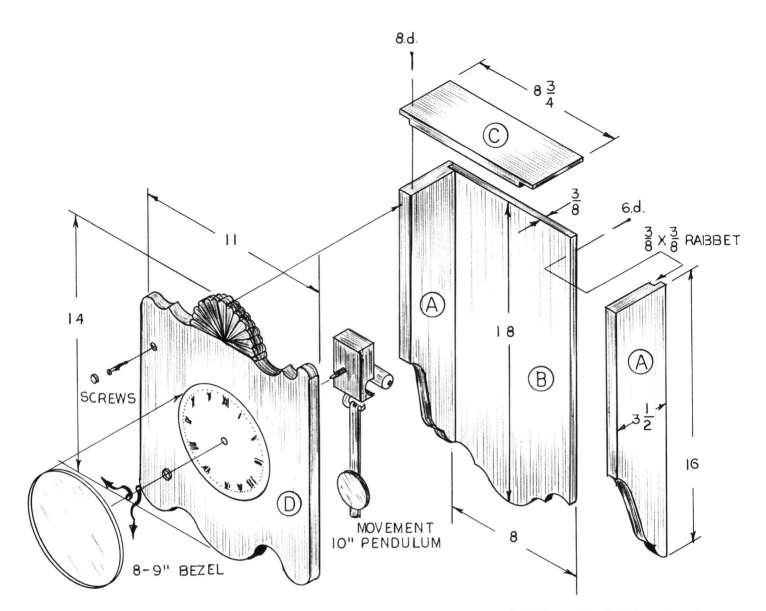

8.d.

8 ¾

C

3/8

6.d.

3/8 X 3/8 RABBET

11

A

18

14

SCREWS

A

3 ½

B

16

D

MOVEMENT
10" PENDULUM

8

8-9" BEZEL

Painted, carved wall clock assembly plan.

SECTION TWO

Shelf Clocks

Carved eagle clock. Index of American Design, National Gallery of Art, Washington, D.C.

Most clocks come under one of three categories: shelf, or "setting," clocks; wall-hanging pieces; or freestanding, floor-type models. Actual size has very little to do with the categories. Some shelf clocks are huge, while some wall clocks are very diminutive.

The book sections that follow were developed and designed around a particular category: shelf, wall, or floor models. The clocks in the following section were all designed as setting, or shelf units. They range widely in size and age, but they all contain the classic lines and timeless beauty sought for in the contents of this book.

Midnight finish, mantel clock.

Classic Mantel Clock
(Late 1800s)

The first mantel clocks were often cased in marble and employed a classic Greek or Roman style. The following reproduction was developed from such antique pieces, but it was modified so that it can be made entirely from wood.

Material List

Part	Number	Size
A Sides	2	4" x 9" x ¾"
B Front	1	9" x 13" x ¾"
C Back	1	9" x 11½" x ½"
D Cove moldings	4	¾" x ¾" x 3¾"
	2	¾" x ¾" x 14½"
E Top/bottom	2	5½" x 16" x ¾"
F Scotia	1	3¼" x 11" x ¾"
G Rosettes	2	2" dia., brass
H Column	1	1⅜" dia. x 7½", cut in half to form two parts
J Feet	4	1¼" x 2½" x ¼"

5¾" dia. bezel/dial combination
Movement of choice
4 brass corner brackets, 1½"–2"

57

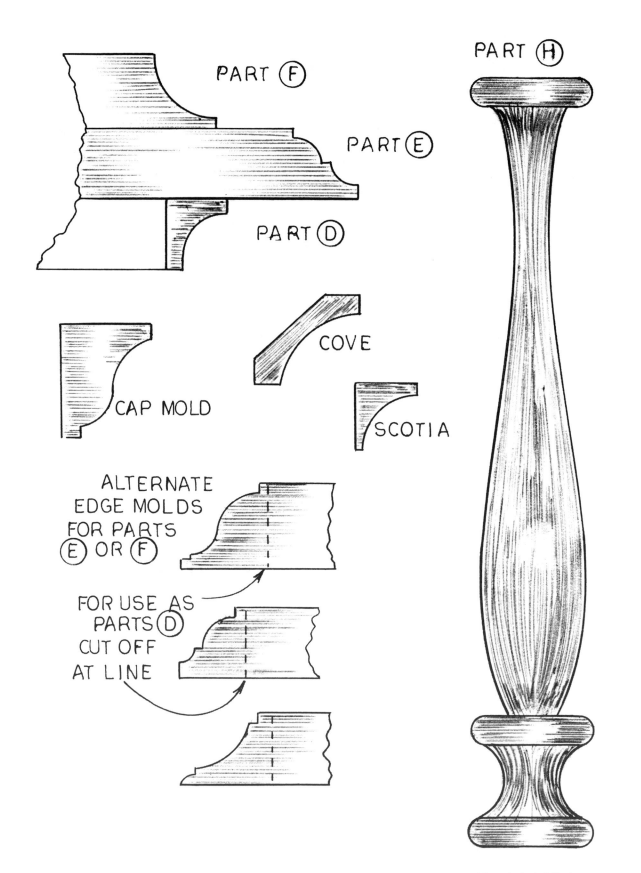

PART F

PART E

PART D

CAP MOLD

COVE

SCOTIA

ALTERNATE
EDGE MOLDS
FOR PARTS
E OR F

FOR USE AS
PARTS D
CUT OFF
AT LINE

PART H

Mantel clock full-size patterns.

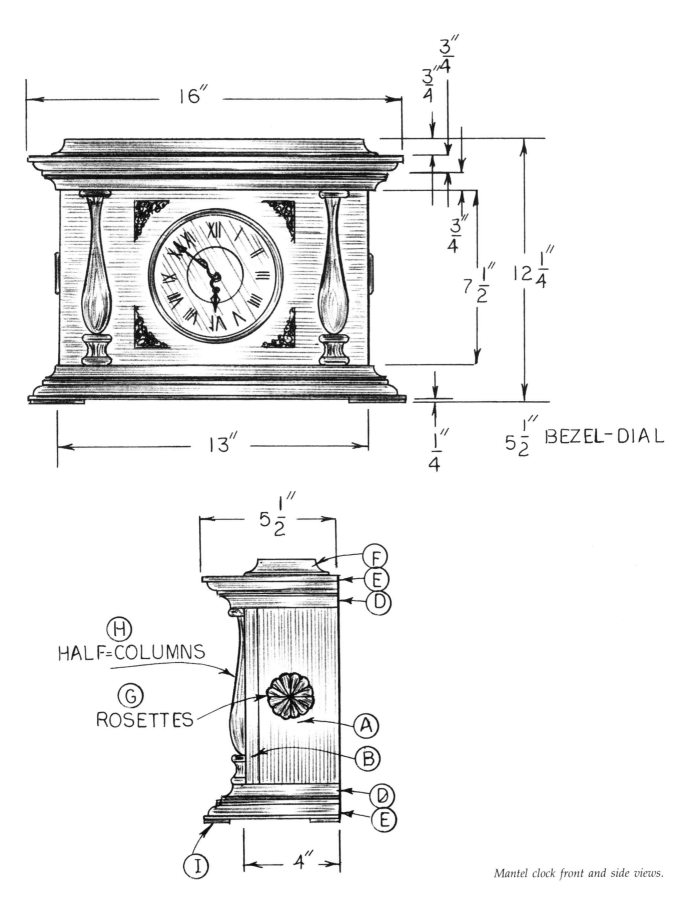

16″

3″/4

3″/4

3″/4

7 1/2″

12 1/4″

13″

1/4″

5 1/2″ BEZEL-DIAL

5 1/2″

F
E
D

H
HALF=COLUMNS

G
ROSETTES

A

B

Ø

E

I

4″

Mantel clock front and side views.

59

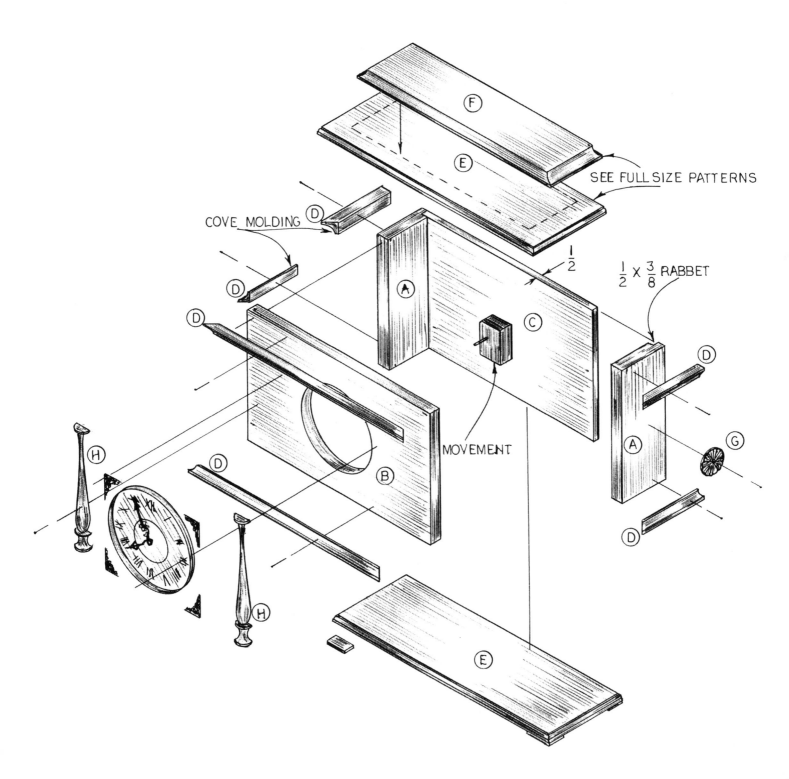

SEE FULL SIZE PATTERNS

COVE MOLDING

MOVEMENT

$\frac{1}{2}$

$\frac{1}{2} \times \frac{3}{8}$ RABBET

Mantel clock assembly plan.

CONSTRUCTION

1. Lay out and cut Parts A, B, C, and E to suggested shape and size. Cut a ½″ x ⅜″ rabbet on the rear inside edges of Parts A. Nail Part B to Parts A. Nail Part C into the rabbets in Parts A. With a router, cut a design on the front and ends of Parts E. (See full-size patterns for suggestions.)

2. Nail or screw Parts E into Parts A, B, and C. Using 45° miter joints, cut the small cove or purchased scotia moldings and nail Parts D into Parts A, B, and E. (See full-size patterns.)

3. Cut Part F to size. With a router, cut a molded design on all four sides. Glue and nail Part F to the top of Part E.

4. Clock columns may be turned on a lathe or purchased from most lumber or hardware outlets. From these make the two half-columns, Parts H. Sand these half-columns to fit between the front cove moldings, Parts D. Glue the columns in place.

5. Mark the location of the clock bezel/dial and cut the required movement seat or recess hole. Secure the movement to the dial and secure the clock hands in place. Secure the assembly to the clock front, Part B. Secure the four decorative corner brackets to Part B. *Note: Access must be obtained to the movement back in order to change batteries and adjust the hands. It is suggested that a small access hole be cut into Part C. The alternative would be to remove the dial/bezel for battery replacement when needed.*

6. Remove dial/bezel, rosettes, and brackets.

Mantel-style clock.
Turncraft Imports Co., Golden Valley, Minnesota.

Set and fill all nailheads. Fill all screwheads with plugs. Sand entire clock smooth. Stain or paint to a color of choice and cover with several coats of lacquer or similar finish. (See Appendix for finishing suggestions.) This clock may be spray-painted with a high-gloss enamel if preferred. The surface may also be marbleized. Replace the bezel/dial, brackets, and rosettes.

Round-top Mantel Clock

Most late 19th-century homes had at least one round-top mantel clock. Clocks of this style are still being made and sold today. The following reproduction was designed to be made from scrap wood of any species.

Material List

Part	Number	Size
A	1	3½" x 9" x 14"
B	1	4¾" x 16" x ¾"
C	4	2½" x 1¼" x ¼"

5½" dia. dial/bezel combination
Small movement of choice

CONSTRUCTION

1. Glue up the stock in order to achieve the suggested thickness of Part A. Trace the pattern of Part A to the glued-up stock and cut it out. Cut a round or square hole in the center of Part A for the movement seat. Battery or hand adjustments can be achieved by means of a hole or opening cut into the back of Part A. Sand Part A smooth.

2. Lay out and cut Part B. With a router, cut a design on the front and both ends. Glue or screw Part B to Part A. Glue and nail the feet to the bottom of Part B.

3. Sand the entire reproduction smooth. Fill all nailheads. Stain or paint to a color of choice. (See Appendix for suggestions.) Many original clocks were stained a very dark mahogany or finished with a high-gloss black enamel.

4. Secure the selected movement to the dial/bezel. Secure the bezel to the center of Part A.

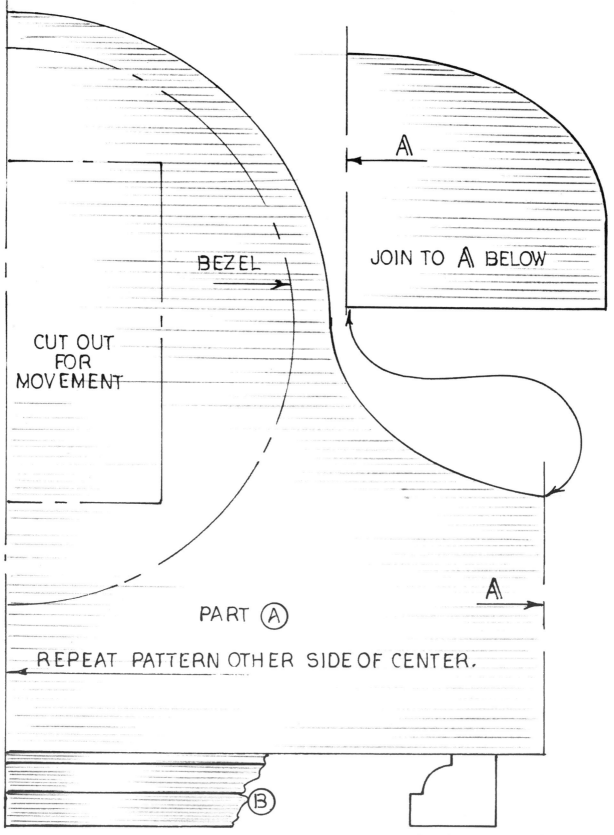

BEZEL

JOIN TO Ⓐ BELOW

CUT OUT
FOR
MOVEMENT

PART Ⓐ

REPEAT PATTERN OTHER SIDE OF CENTER.

Ⓑ

Round-top mantel clock full-size patterns.

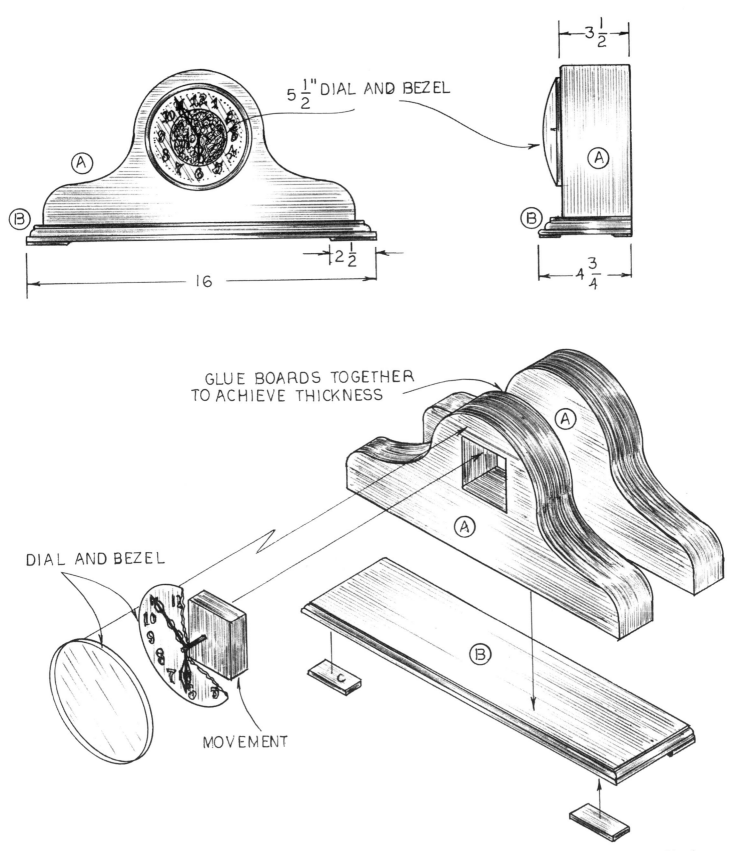

$5\frac{1}{2}$" DIAL AND BEZEL

$3\frac{1}{2}$

Ⓐ

Ⓑ

$4\frac{3}{4}$

Ⓐ

Ⓑ

$2\frac{1}{2}$

16

GLUE BOARDS TOGETHER
TO ACHIEVE THICKNESS

Ⓐ

Ⓐ

DIAL AND BEZEL

Ⓑ

c

MOVEMENT

Round-top mantel clock assembly plan.

Gable-end Shelf Clock

Many old clocks were shaped to resemble little houses. Some had steeples, roofs, balconies, doors, and windows. The following clock is a composite of several antique pieces still in existence.

Material List

Part	Number	Size
A Sides	2	4" x 14½" x ¾"
B Base	1	6½" x 14" x ¾"
C Roof	2	6½" x 8" x ¾"
D Back	1	10¼" x 18" x ½"
E Door	1	11" x 17¼" x ¾"
F Column (2 halves)	1	1½" dia. x 14"

Round 8" dia. dial

Movement of choice with 8" pendulum

CONSTRUCTION

1. Lay out and cut the stock for Parts A, B, C, and D. Cut a ⅜" x ½" rabbet into the rear inside edges of Parts A. With a router, cut a molded edge on Parts B and C. (See assembly drawing for suggestions.) Cut a 30° angle on the tops of Parts A.

2. Secure Part B to Parts A with nails or screws. Nail Part D into the rabbets cut into Parts A. Nail Parts C together and into Parts A and D.

3. Make or purchase a turned column. Split the column in half and glue one half to each Part A, between Parts B and C. *Note: In order to achieve a perfect half-split on turnings, do the following. Glue up two pieces of stock with a piece of newspaper in between them. Spread glue on both pieces of stock, insert the paper, and clamp them under pressure until the glue has dried. When the turning design is completed, gently pry the two halves apart at the paper joint. The column should split perfectly along this paper joint. The paper is then removed and the half-columns glued in place on the clock.*

4. Make a door with a half-round top rail. This half-circle should be centered where the round dial will be placed in order to frame the dial. The door is made with butt, spline, or dowel joints. Rout a molded edge on the inside edges. Cut a glass rabbet on the inside rear edges. Secure glass in the rabbet using thin quarter-round wood strips. Secure the right-hand side of the door to Part A with 1" x 1" brass hinges. Install a catch and door pull.

5. Set and fill all nailheads. Cover all screwheads with plugs. Sand entire reproduction smooth. Stain to a color of choice and cover with several coats of lacquer or similar finish. (See Appendix under *Finishing* for suggestions.) Install the movement and selected dial. A dial frame or backer may be required.

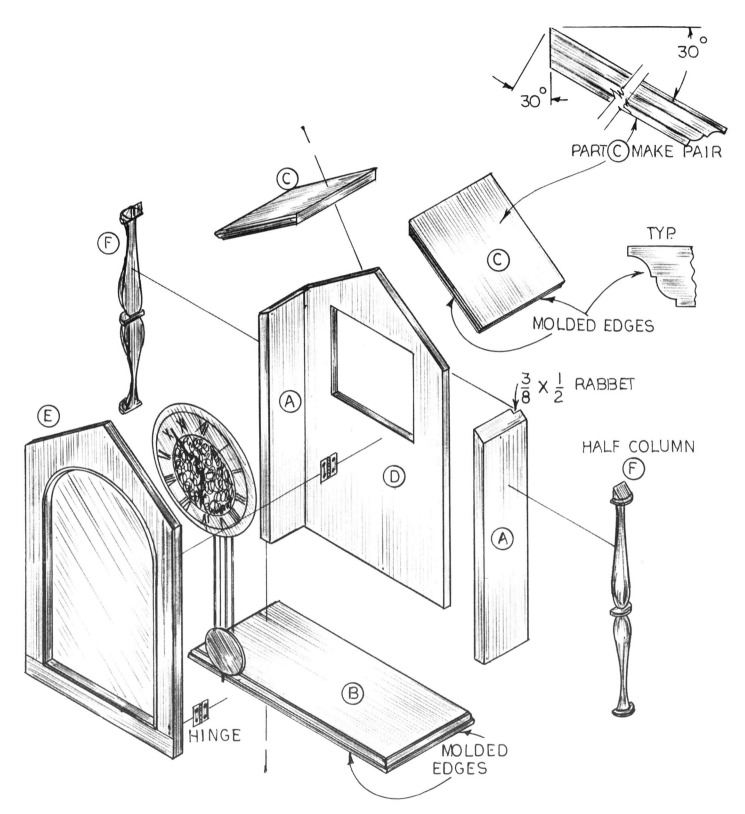

30°   30°

PART Ⓒ MAKE PAIR

TYP.

Ⓒ

Ⓒ

MOLDED EDGES

Ⓕ

$\frac{3}{8} \times \frac{1}{2}$ RABBET

Ⓐ

HALF COLUMN

Ⓕ

Ⓔ

Ⓐ

Ⓓ

Ⓐ

HINGE

Ⓑ

MOLDED
EDGES

Gable end shelf clock assembly plan.

66

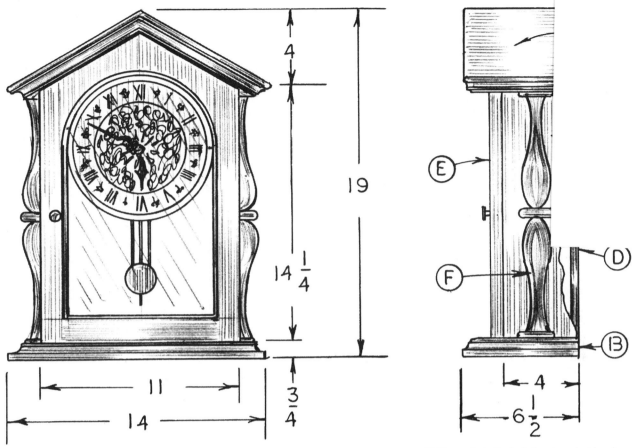

Gable end shelf clock front and side views.

Carriage clock, pine.

Carriage Clock

Many original carriage clocks were imported from England, where they were made in great numbers during our colonial days. American clockmakers began to exploit the popularity of the carriage-style clock, and many examples are now on display in museums.

Material List

Part		Number	Size
A	Sides	2	4″ x 12¾″ x ¾″
B	Back	1	9¾″ x 13½″ x ⅝″
C	Top	1	5¾″ x 12½″ x ¾″
D	Bottom	1	5¾″ x 12½″ x ¾″
E	Crown	1	2″ x 10½″ x 4″
F	Backer	1	9″ x 12¾″ x ⅜″
G	Door bottom rail	1	1¼″ x 10½″ x ¾″
	Door top rail	1	3½″ x 10½″ x ¾″
	Door stiles	2	1¼″ x 12¾″ x ¾″
H	Feet	4	1″ x 2″ x ¼″

7⅞″ x 10½″ dial with moon or decorative arch
Movement of choice
Glass or Plexiglas panel

CONSTRUCTION

1. Lay out and cut the stock to suggested shape and size. Cut a ⅜″ x ⅜″ rabbet into the rear inside edges of Parts A. With a router or shaper, mold the edges of Parts C and D. Mark on Parts C and D the location for Parts A. Drill screw pilot holes into Parts C and D. Screw Parts C and D into Parts A. Fit Part B into the rabbets cut in Parts A. Cut a raised panel design into Part B. (See assembly drawing detail.) Secure Part B into the rabbets in Parts A with small brads.

2. Cut the crown molding, Part E, to size and shape. Part E can be made from a solid block or from crown molding cut with 45° corner miters. Secure Part E to the top of Part C with nails. Cut the dial backer, Part F, to shape and size so that it fits into Parts A, C, and D. Secure this piece ½″ back from the front edges of Parts A. Small nail blocks should be used as cleats. Nail Parts H to the bottom corners of Part D.

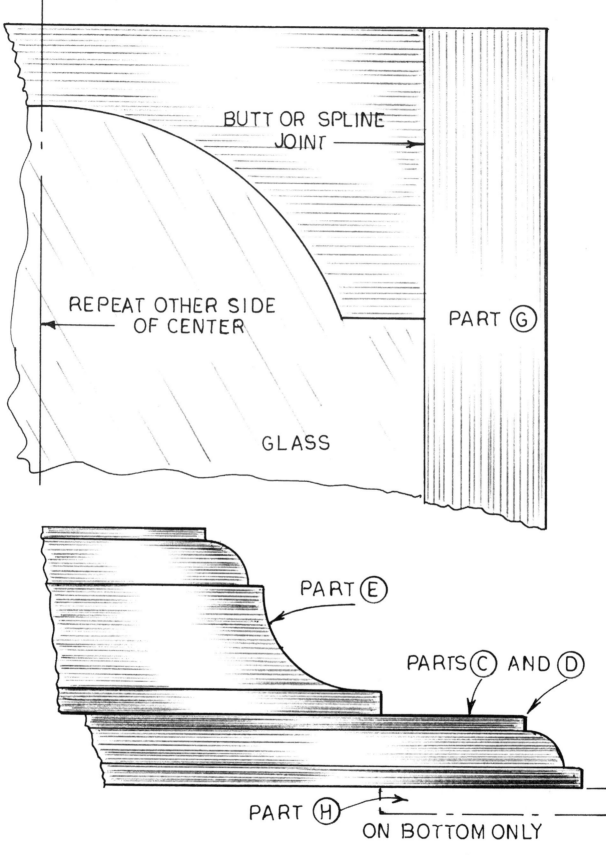

BUTT OR SPLINE JOINT

REPEAT OTHER SIDE OF CENTER

GLASS

PART G

PART E

PARTS C AND D

PART H   ON BOTTOM ONLY

Carriage clock full-size patterns.

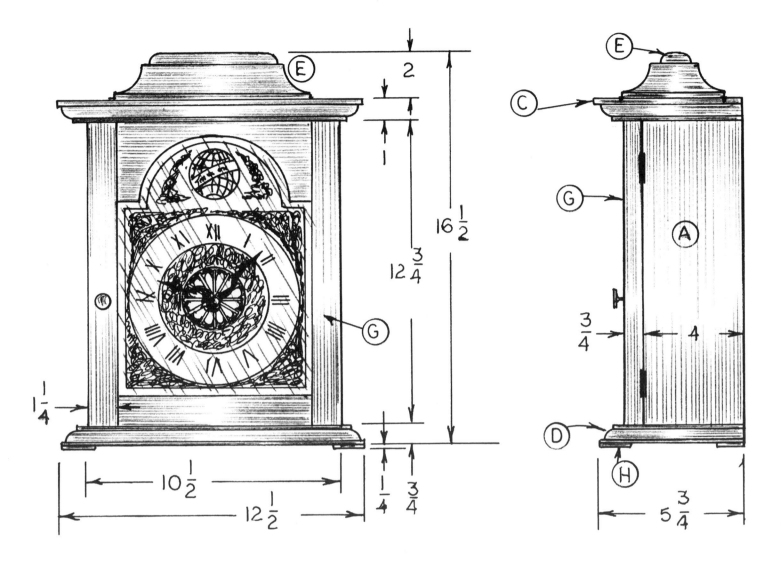

Carriage clock front and side views.

3. Lay out and construct a door, Part G, to suggested size and shape. (See full-size patterns for suggestions.) Use butt, spline, or dowel joints for construction. Cut a ¼″ x ¼″ rabbet into the rear inside edges of the finished door. Install the glass in this rabbet with glazier's points or wood stops. Install the completed door to the right-hand Part A with 1″ x 1″ brass butt hinges.

4. Set and fill all nailheads. Cover all screwheads with plugs. Stain to a color of choice. (See Appendix under *Finishing* for suggestions.)

5. This carriage clock was designed to take a 7⅞″ wide by 10½″ high dial using either a moving moon dial or a decorated arch. Install the movement of your choice in the center of the selected dial. Cut a relief hole in the center of Part F. Install the movement/dial to Part F. Install the hands over the hand shaft.

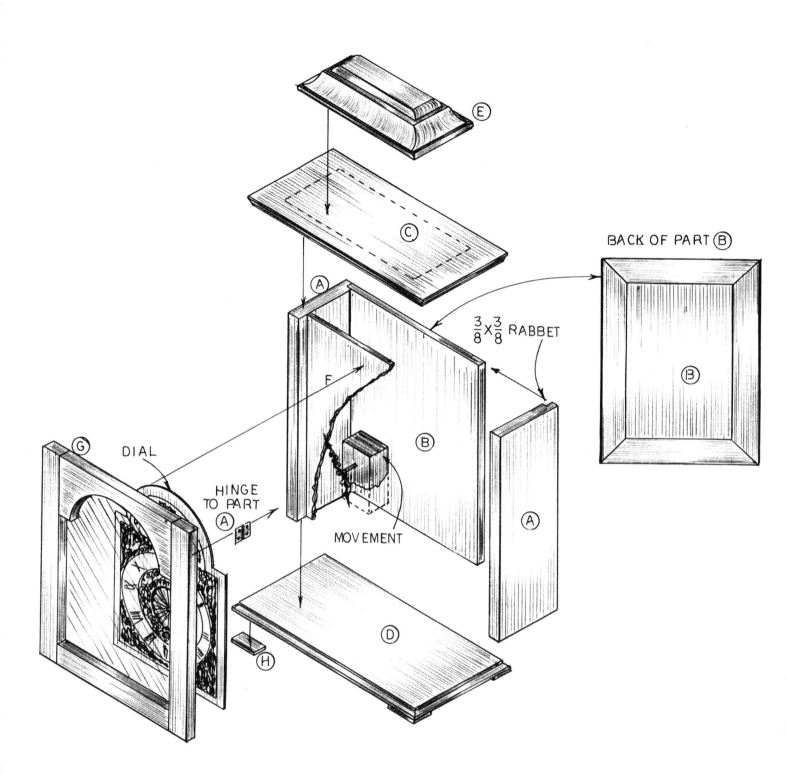

BACK OF PART Ⓑ

$\frac{3}{8} \times \frac{3}{8}$ RABBET

Ⓔ

Ⓒ

Ⓐ

Ⓑ

F

Ⓑ

Ⓐ

Ⓖ

DIAL

HINGE
TO PART
Ⓐ

MOVEMENT

Ⓗ

Ⓓ

Carriage clock assembly plan.

Carriage-style clock, Colonial Williamsburg.

Colonial Bracket Clock

The bracket clock and the later-period carriage clock look very similar. While the bracket clock uses a square dial and is cornered by four decorative brackets, the basic design is the same as that of the carriage clock.

Material List

Part		Number	Size
A	Sides	2	4″ x 10″ x ¾″
B	Back	1	9¼″ x 9¼″ x ¾″
C	Top/bottom	2	5¾″ x 12″ x ¾″
D	Molding*	1	3″ x 8″ x 2½″
E	Dial backer	1	8½″ x 8½″ x ⅜″
F	Door	1	10″ x 10″ x ¾″
G	Feet	4	1¼″ x 1¼″ x ¼″

7⅞″ (200mm) square dial with decorative side brackets
Movement of choice
Bail-type door pull or handle

*Regular lumberyard crown molding may be used if desired, with the part made up by using mitered corner joints.

CONSTRUCTION

1. Lay out and cut Parts A, B, and C to shape and size. Cut a ⅜″ x ⅜″ rabbet on the rear inside edges on Parts A and blind rabbets on Parts C. (A blind rabbet is a groove that does not extend through to the end of the part.) Rout a molded edge on Parts C. (See assembly drawing for raised-panel design for the back piece.) Nail or screw Parts C to Parts A. Nail Part B into the rabbets in Parts A and C.

2. Make or purchase the molding for the top, Part D. Molding will require 45° miter cuts on the corners. Secure a bail-type handle or pull to the center of the molding assembly. Secure the molded cap to the top, Part C. Nail Part E in place, ½″ back from the front edges of Parts A. Cut a movement access hole or seat in the dial backer piece.

3. Make a door of 1″ wide stiles and rails using half-lap-end joinery. Rout glass rabbets

Colonial-style bracket clock, pine with brass dial.

on the rear inside edges of this door. Secure the glass panel into the rabbets using glazier's points or thin wood strips. Attach the door to the right-hand Part A using 1" x 1" brass butt hinges. Nail the four feet, Parts G, to the bottom of Part C.

4. Set and fill all nailheads. Cover all screwheads with hardwood plugs. Sand entire reproduction smooth. Stain or paint to a color of choice. Cover with several coats of lacquer or similar finish. *Note: Some very old clocks were painted and not stained. Red, green, yellow, and blue were some of the colors used. Other models were stained a very dark color. (See Appendix under* Finishing *for suggestions on various techniques.)* Attach the movement to the selected dial or in its backer seat. Attach the dial, centered, within the glass panel area of the doorframe.

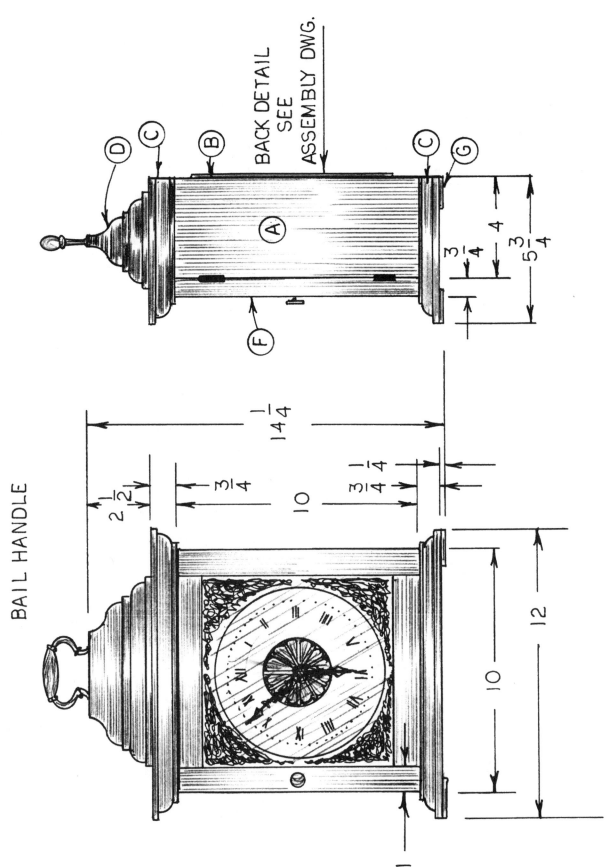

BAIL HANDLE

BACK DETAIL
SEE
ASSEMBLY DWG.

Ⓓ Ⓒ Ⓑ Ⓒ Ⓖ Ⓕ Ⓐ

$3\frac{1}{4}$

4

$5\frac{3}{4}$

$14\frac{1}{4}$

$2\frac{1}{2}$

$\frac{3}{4}$

10

$3\frac{1}{4}$

12

10

1

Colonial bracket clock front and side views.

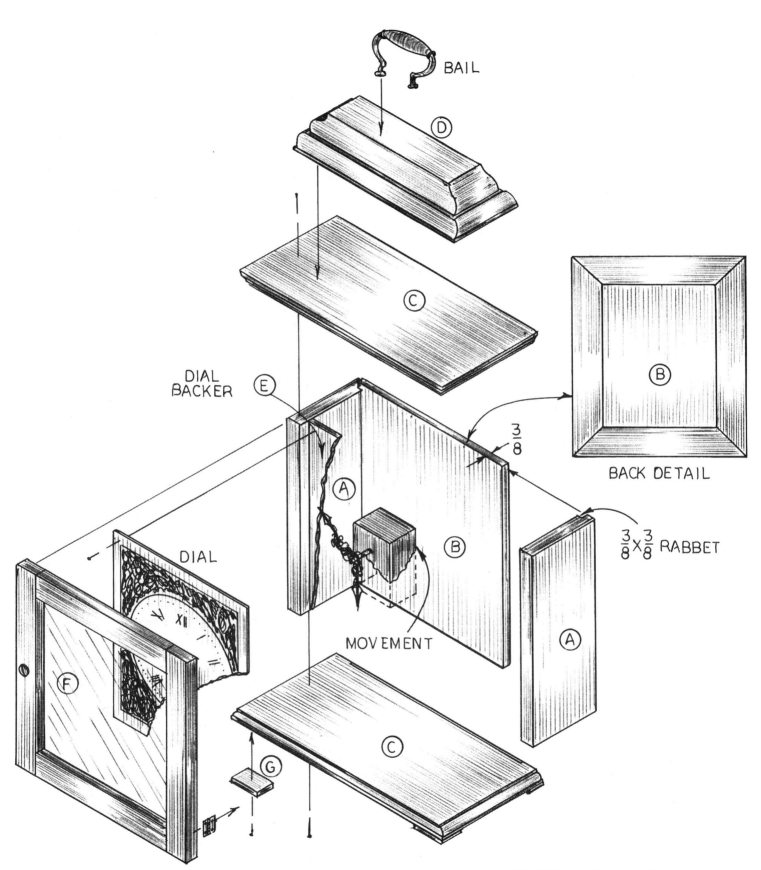

BAIL

D

BACK DETAIL

B

3/8

3/8 X 3/8 RABBET

DIAL BACKER

E

C

A

B

MOVEMENT

DIAL

F

A

C

G

Colonial bracket clock assembly plan.

Steeple Clock (Circa mid-1800s)

Steeple clock.
Turncraft Clock Imports Co., Golden Valley, Minnesota.

Some authorities claim the steeple clock is of American design, built upon classic Gothic lines. At times the clock front, with its highly artistic painted panel and floral designs on the dial, gives the effect of a church stained-glass window.

There are as many different styles of steeple clocks as there were clockmakers. Each worker had a favorite design, and hundreds of these clocks are still ticking away in private collections or museums. The following reproduction was developed from several antique pieces displayed at Old Sturbridge Village, Sturbridge, Massachusetts.

Material List

Part	Number	Size
A Sides	2	3½″ x 8¾″ x ¾″
B Roof	2	3½″ x 8″ x ¾″
C Back	1	7¼″ x 14¾″ x ⅜″
D Base	1	5½″ x 10″ x ¾″
E Door	4	1″ x 8″ x ¾″
	1	2″ x 6″ x ¾″
	1	¾″ x 6″ x ¾″
F Steeple	2	1″ x 1″ x 1¼″

Steeple-style dial (6″ x 8″ is typical)
Movement of choice with short pendulum
Decorated glass panel (3″ x 6½″ is typical; decal may be used if preferred)
Clear glass panel for door (6½″ x 9″ is typical)

CONSTRUCTION

1. Lay out and cut Parts A and B. Note angles in full-size patterns. Cut a ⅜″ x ⅜″ rabbet on rear inside edges of Parts A and B. Secure Parts B together and secure to Parts A. It will prove helpful to lay out a full-size paper pattern of the angle cuts and seats and fasten the pieces together along the pattern lines. Lay out and

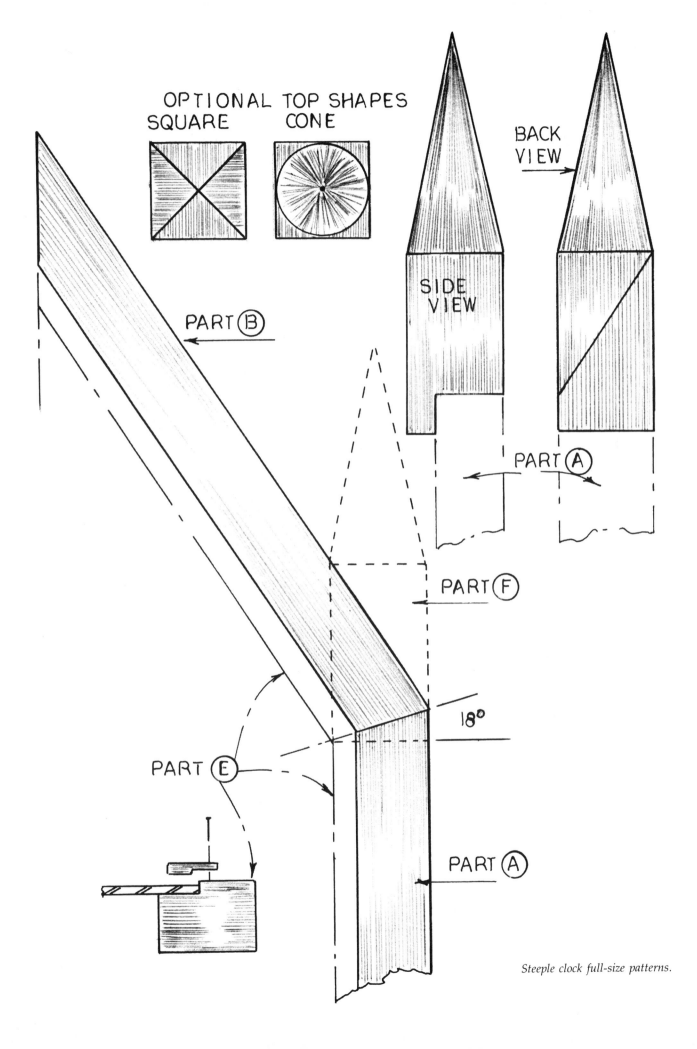

OPTIONAL TOP SHAPES
SQUARE   CONE

BACK VIEW

PART B

SIDE VIEW

PART A

PART F

18°

PART E

PART A

Steeple clock full-size patterns.

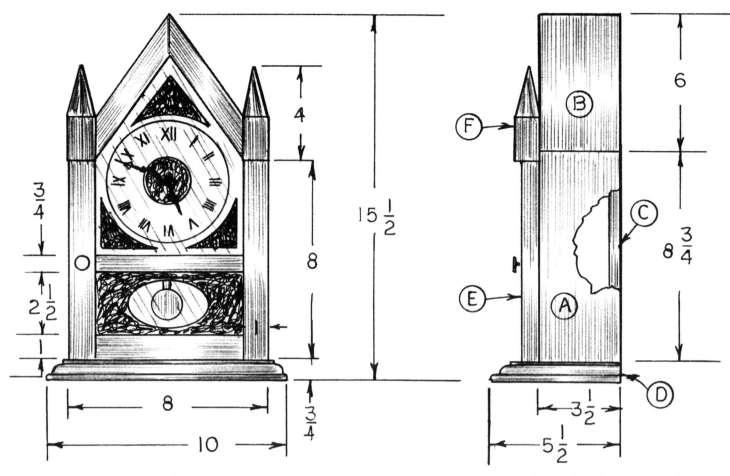

Steeple clock front and side views.

cut Parts C and D to shape and size. Nail Part C into the rabbets in Parts A and B. Cut a molded edge on Part D. Screw Part D into Parts A and C.

2. Make a dial seat or cleat frame and attach it to Parts A and B, ½" back from the front edges. This frame or cleat arrangement will help secure Parts A and B togther at their weakest points. If a solid wood backer is used, cut the movement access hole in the center of the peaked area.

3. Make a door using spline or dowel joints. The door should perfectly match the size and angles of Parts A and B. Cut a glass rabbet in the rear inside edges of the door. Make two steeple pieces, Parts F. Steeple pieces and full angle cuts are shown in full-size patterns. Glue

Parts F to the door at the junction of the peak pieces. (See location in the full-size pattern plan.) Attach the door to the right-hand Part A with 1" x 1" brass butt hinges. Attach a door catch and a small door pull.

4. Set and fill all nailheads. Cover all screwheads with plugs. Sand entire clock smooth. Stain or paint to a color of choice. (See Appendix for suggestions.) Cover with several coats of lacquer or similar finish.

5. Install the movement in its recess or to the dial. Install the decorative glass panel in the door bottom glass rabbets. Install the clear glass panel in the door top glass rabbets. Hold the glass in place with glazier's points or thin wood strips. Install the dial and secure it to the dial backer.

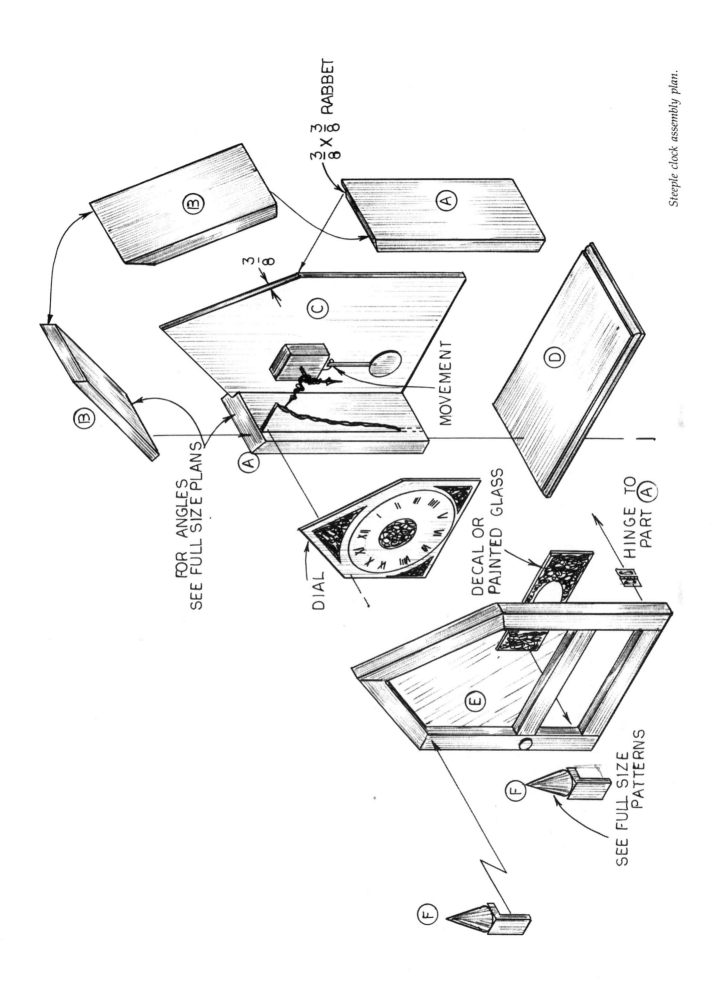

$\frac{3}{8} \times \frac{3}{8}$ RABBET

$\frac{3}{8}$

Ⓐ

Ⓑ

Ⓒ

Ⓑ

Ⓐ

Ⓓ

MOVEMENT

FOR ANGLES
SEE FULL SIZE PLANS

DIAL

DECAL OR
PAINTED GLASS

Ⓔ

HINGE TO
PART Ⓐ

SEE FULL SIZE
PATTERNS

Ⓕ

Ⓕ

Steeple clock assembly plan.

Steeple clock. Author's collection.

Pillar and Scroll Clock (also known as Terry Pillar and Scroll) (Circa 1808)

This pillar and scroll clock is an American classic. The original clock was designed and made by Eli Terry around 1808, and several hundred imitations and copies were made by clockmakers all over the world.

The charm of the clock rests with the floral designs worked into the dial corners; the floral, scenic, or scroll design of the bottom glass panel; the three brass finials; the swan-neck pediment; and the turned columns.

The following reproduction was developed from several prototypes found in museums.

Material List

Part	Number	Size
A Back	1	13½″ x 16½″ x ¾″
B Sides	2	4¾″ x 16½″ x ¾″
C Top	1	6¾″ x 15½″ x ¾″
D Base	1	6¾″ x 15½″ x ¾″
E Front skirts	1	2½″ x 13½″ x ½″
F Side skirts	2	2½″ x 6″ x ½″
G Swan-neck	1	4½″ x 12″ x ½″
H Side molding	2	1½″ x 4½″ x ½″
I Finials	3	1¼″ dia. x 3″
J Columns	2	1″ dia. x 16½″
K Door	1	10½″ x 16½″ x ¾″

7⅞″ (200mm) square dial, floral corner designs
Terry-style decal or painted glass panel
Movement of choice with 6″ pendulum
Clear glass panel for door top

CONSTRUCTION

1. Lay out and cut Parts A, B, C, and D to shape and size. Cut a molded edge on both ends of Part A. Screw Part A into Parts B. (See full-size patterns for location and number.) Screw Parts C and D into Parts A and B.

2. Lay out and cut Parts E and F to shape and size. (See full-size patterns for designs.) Make 45° miter corner on these parts. Screw Parts E and F to the bottom of Part D.

3. Lay out and cut Parts G and H to shape and size. (See full-size patterns for suggestions.) Screw Parts G and H to the top of Part C. Make or purchase finials. Secure the finials to Parts G and H.

4. Make or purchase the turned columns, Parts J. The columns should have a tenon on each end. Mortise holes are drilled into Parts C and D, and the column tenons are inserted into these holes. In order to do this, Part C or D will have to be removed, the holes drilled, columns inserted, and the parts replaced. Make a door using 1¼″ wide stiles and rails. Use dowel, half-lap, butt, or spline joinery. Rout a molded edge on the inside edges of this door-frame. (See full-size pattern for detail.) Rout a glass rabbet on the rear inside edges of the door.

Pillar and scroll clock. Author's collection.

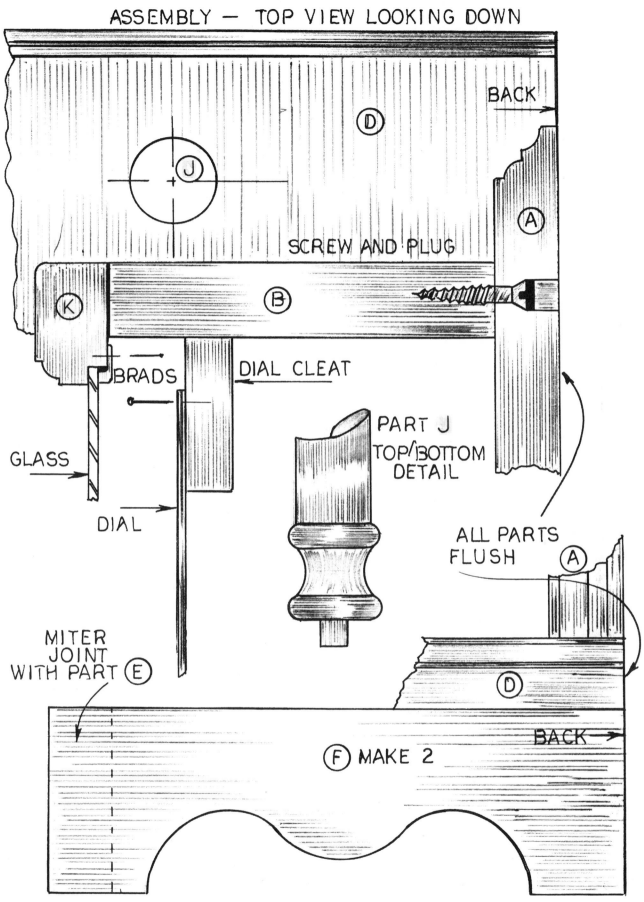

ASSEMBLY — TOP VIEW LOOKING DOWN

BACK

Ⓓ

Ⓐ

SCREW AND PLUG

Ⓚ

Ⓑ

BRADS

DIAL CLEAT

GLASS

DIAL

PART J
TOP/BOTTOM
DETAIL

ALL PARTS
FLUSH

Ⓐ

Ⓓ

BACK

MITER
JOINT
WITH PART Ⓔ

Ⓕ MAKE 2

Pillar and scroll clock full-size patterns.

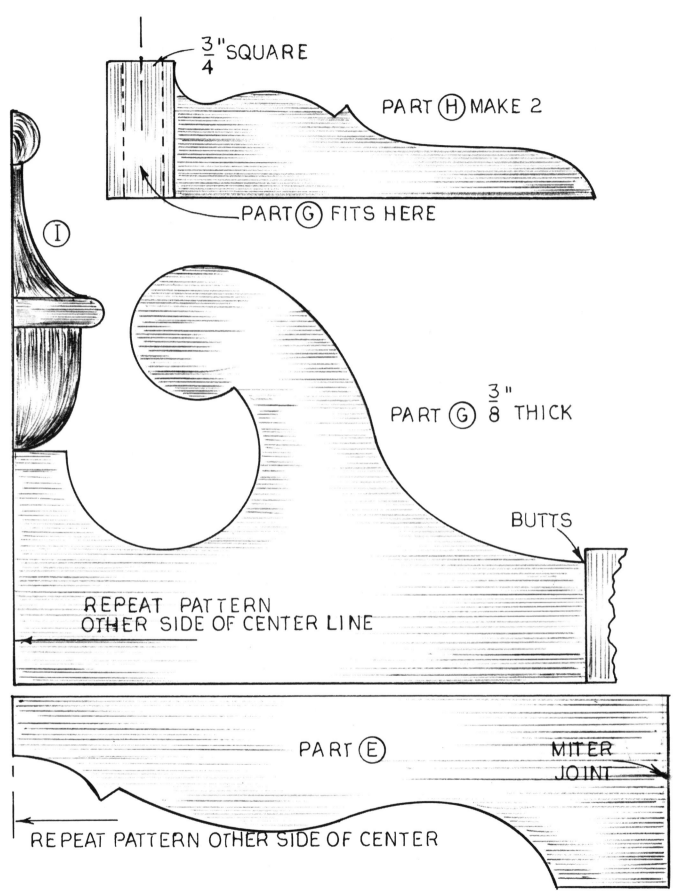

3/4" SQUARE

PART (H) MAKE 2

PART (G) FITS HERE

(I)

PART (G) 3/8" THICK

BUTTS

REPEAT PATTERN
OTHER SIDE OF CENTER LINE

PART (E)

MITER JOINT

REPEAT PATTERN OTHER SIDE OF CENTER

Pillar and scroll clock full-size patterns.

86

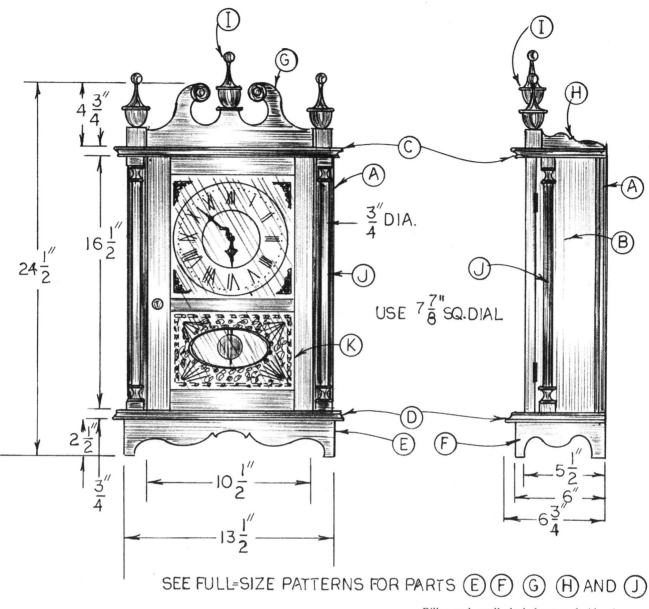

SEE FULL-SIZE PATTERNS FOR PARTS Ⓔ Ⓕ Ⓖ Ⓗ AND Ⓙ

Pillar and scroll clock front and side views.

Install a clear glass panel in the top door section and a painted or decal-covered decorative glass panel in the door's bottom section. Secure the door to the right-hand Part B, using 1½" x 1½" brass butt hinges.

5. Make a dial frame or cleat seat for the dial, and install this frame ½" back from the front edges of Parts B. Cut an access hole for the movement if required. Install the movement and the dial.

6. Set and fill all nailheads. Cover all screw-heads with plugs–except those in Part D, so the clock can be taken apart if needed. Sand entire clock smooth. Stain to a color of choice and cover with several coats of lacquer or similar finish. (See Appendix under *Finishing* for suggestions.) Reinstall the movement, glass, and dial.

Note: While this clock was designed as a shelf or mantel clock, I have placed mine on a small shelf mounted to a wall. (See instructions and patterns for a clock wall shelf in the next section.)

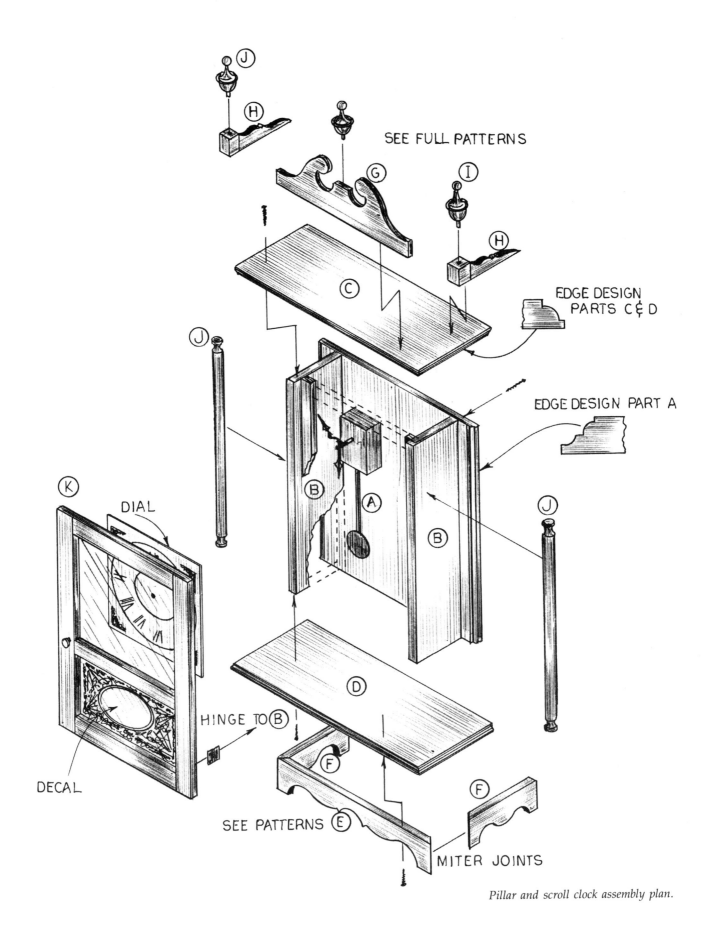

SEE FULL PATTERNS

EDGE DESIGN PARTS C & D

EDGE DESIGN PART A

DIAL

HINGE TO (B)

DECAL

SEE PATTERNS (E)

MITER JOINTS

Pillar and scroll clock assembly plan.

SECTION THREE

Wall Clocks

Antique clocks. Old Sturbridge Village, Sturbridge, Massachusetts.

Laying out a crown arc molding. Top left, *lay out the design or arc and remove lower excess wood;* center left, *rout the selected design and cut the top arc, freeing the molded piece from the holding block;* lower left, *cut a matching top crown or arc on the proposed fascia piece; glue the molded arc in place;* right, *finish crown molded fascia mounted on clock case.*

MAKING MOLDED PEDIMENTS

Several clocks require a molded pediment, swan-neck, or an arched or crowned top design. Since curved or arched moldings are very difficult to find, the following procedure was developed in order to achieve professional-type results using a router and miter box.

1. Lay out the desired arc or shape on a piece of selected stock. (See drawings.) The lower proposed molded edge is cut out first, leaving a large proposed scrap area for working, holding, or clamping. File and sand smooth the cut-out arch or design.

2. With a hand-held router and selected bit, cut in the selected design on the arch or curve. It is recommended that the same design be cut into a section of straight stock that will be used

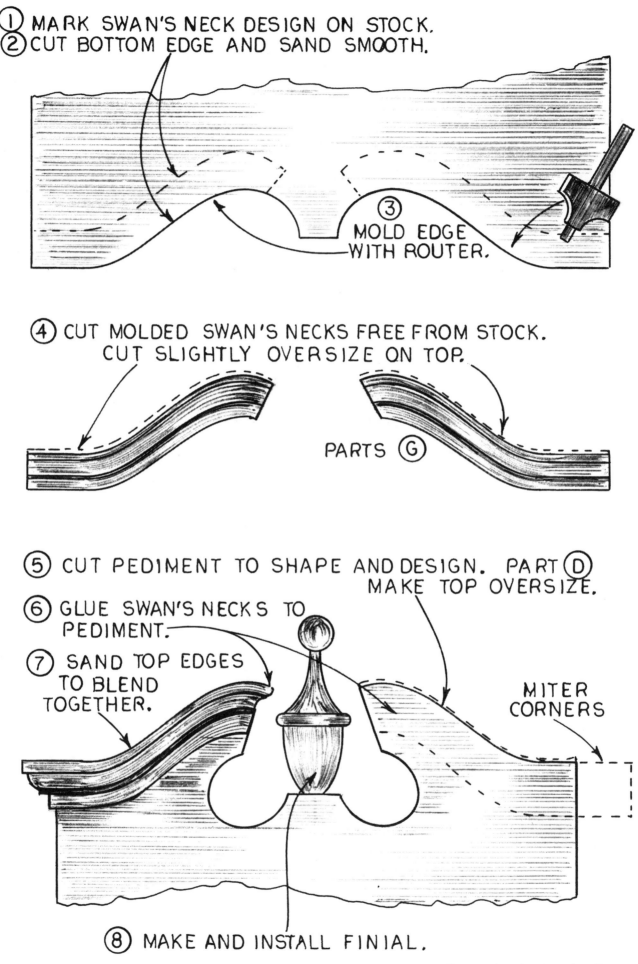

① MARK SWAN'S NECK DESIGN ON STOCK.
② CUT BOTTOM EDGE AND SAND SMOOTH.

③ MOLD EDGE WITH ROUTER.

④ CUT MOLDED SWAN'S NECKS FREE FROM STOCK. CUT SLIGHTLY OVERSIZE ON TOP.

PARTS Ⓖ

⑤ CUT PEDIMENT TO SHAPE AND DESIGN. PART Ⓓ MAKE TOP OVERSIZE.

⑥ GLUE SWAN'S NECKS TO PEDIMENT.

⑦ SAND TOP EDGES TO BLEND TOGETHER.

MITER CORNERS

⑧ MAKE AND INSTALL FINIAL.

Construction of swan-neck pediments.

on the sides or for returns. (See drawings.)

3. Sand the molded cut edge smooth and lay out the top curve or design. Most of the proposed, add-on, molding is 1" to 1¼" wide. (See drawings.) Cut out the top curve or design, leaving the outline on the stock for future sanding.

4. Trace the top molded design onto the home or fascia piece and cut out this design, allowing the outline to remain for future sanding. Cut out any other design required on the home or fascia piece. Sand the face of this piece smooth and glue the molded arc or crown piece(s) in place. After the glue has dried, sand the two pieces (fascia piece and molded arcs), blending them together. The combined finished fascia piece is then attached to the clock case as suggested for the various units.

Wall shelf finished for the pillar and scroll clock.

Clock Wall Shelf, Colonial Design (Late 1700s)

This shelf is designed to hold any clock offered in this book, even a wall clock. The shelf is long enough so that it can be secured directly into house wall studs spaced at the normal 16" on centers. If house studs are not available, expansion-type fasteners may be used to fasten the unit to the plaster wall.

Material List

Part	Number	Size
A Backer	1	3½" x 17½" x ¾"
B Bracket	2	3½" x 4½" x ½"
C Shelf	1	6" x 18"–20" x ¾"

94

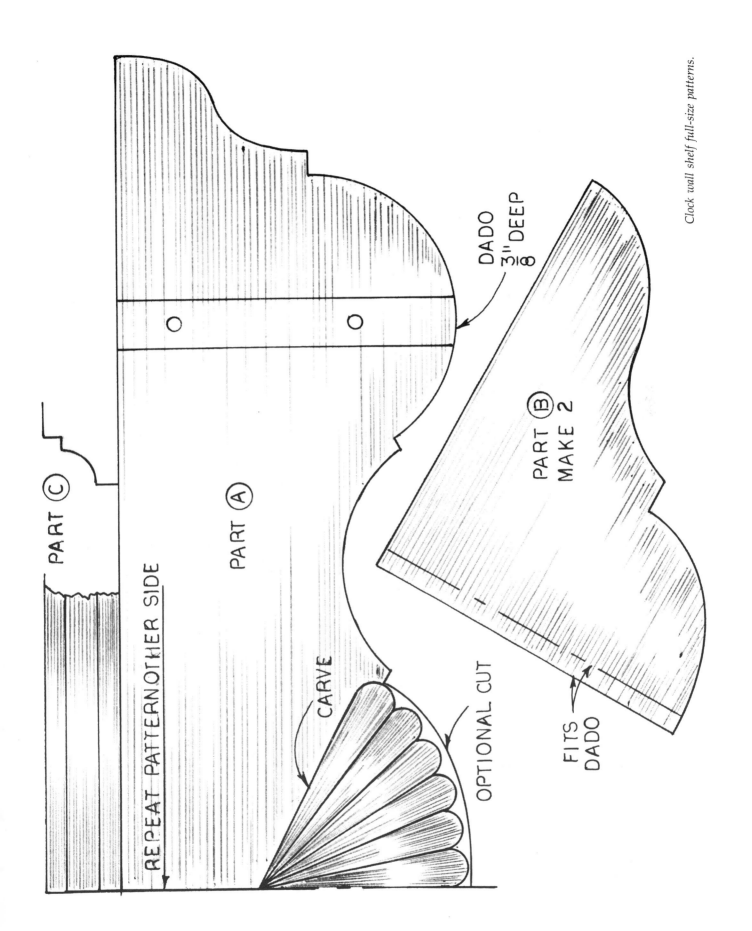

PART Ⓒ

PART Ⓐ

REPEAT PATTERN OTHER SIDE

CARVE

OPTIONAL CUT

DADO
$\frac{3}{8}$" DEEP

PART Ⓑ
MAKE 2

FITS
DADO

Clock wall shelf full-size patterns.

● SCREW AND PLUG.

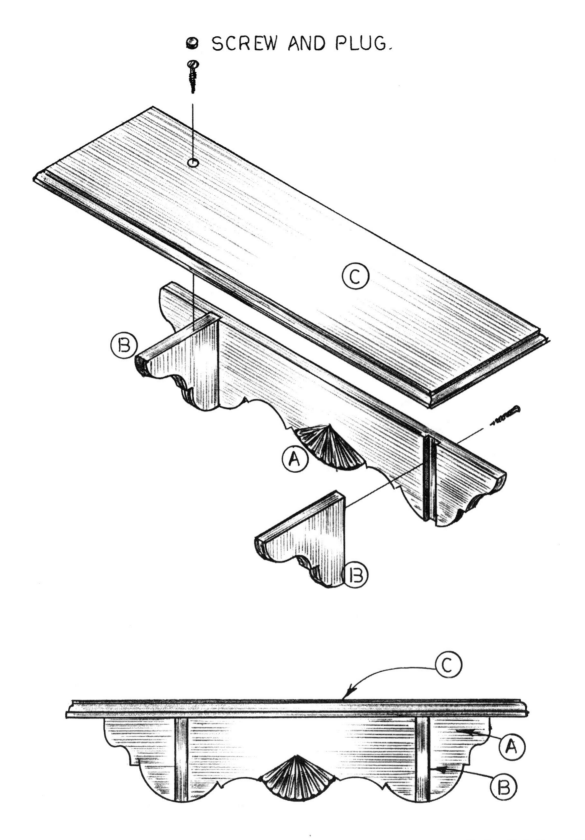

Clock wall shelf assembly plan.

96

CONSTRUCTION

1. Lay out and cut Parts A and B to suggested shape and size. (See full-size patterns.) Cut a ⅜″ deep x ½″ wide dado into Part A as marked. Drill the suggested screw pilot holes in this dado area. (See pattern.) With a set of carving chisels, mat knife, or X-acto knife, cut the shell design into Part A. Sand this design smooth. Screw Part A into both Parts B.

2. Cut the shelf, Part C, to desired shape and size. Part C can be 5″–7″ wide and 18″–22″ long. With a router, cut a design on the front and ends. Screw Part C to Parts A and B.

3. Cover all screwheads with plugs. Sand shelf smooth. Finish the clock shelf to match the reproduction it will support.

Ogee, or Picture Frame, Clock (Circa early 1800s)

The name of this clock comes from the style of molding used for the doorframe. Seth Thomas and other clockmakers built clocks of this type during the 1800s, and the design quickly became a favorite. Much of the clock's beauty comes from the highly molded doorframe and the decorated lower glass panel.

The following reproduction was developed from several models located in museums.

Material List

Part	Number	Size
A Sides	2	4¼" x 24" x ¾"
B Ends	2	4¼" x 13" x ¾"
C Back	1	12¼" x 23¼" x ⅜"
D Door*	1	13". x 24" x ¾"

7⅞" (200mm) square dial
Decorated glass panel 8½" x 13", or decal
Movement of choice with pendulum
Plain glass panel, 8½" x 8½"

*See full-size patterns for suggestions on moldings to use for doorframe construction. Molded frames require 45° miter joints.

CONSTRUCTION

1. Lay out and cut Parts A and B to size. Cut a ⅜" x ⅜" rabbet on the rear inside edges. Using 45° miter joints on Parts A and B, form a box by nailing sides and ends together. Cut Part C to shape and size to fit into the rabbets cut into Parts A and B. Nail Part C into these rabbets.

2. Make a door unit, Part D. This door must match the overall exterior size of the box formed by Parts A, B, and C. It is suggested that the door unit be made slightly larger than the box size and then planed and sanded into a final perfect, matching fit. You might find a standard molding in a lumberyard, or shop-made ogee molding may be used if preferred. A typical width of molded rails and stiles would be 2½". Cut a glass rabbet on the rear inside edges of this doorframe. Secure the door to Part A with 1¼" x 1¼" brass butt hinges. Install a catch and pull.

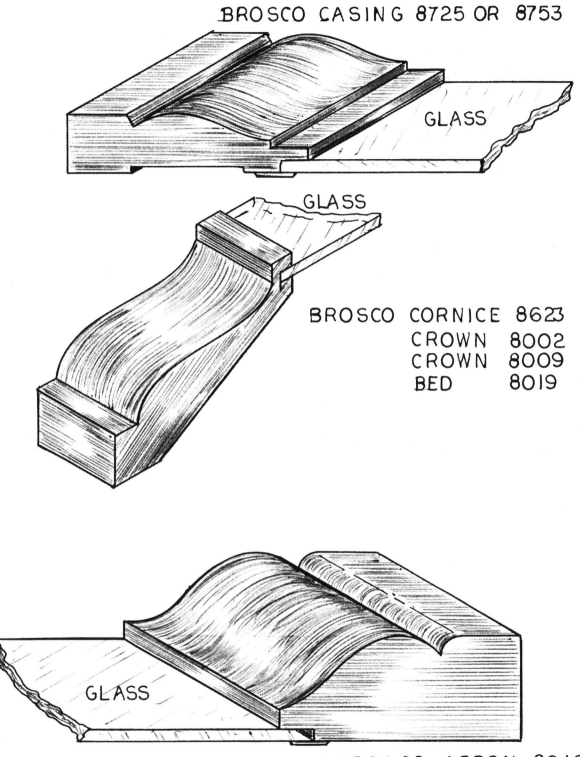

BROSCO CASING 8725 OR 8753

GLASS

GLASS

BROSCO CORNICE 8623
CROWN 8002
CROWN 8009
BED 8019

GLASS

BROSCO APRON 8642A
BROSCO FLAT CROWN 8047

Ogee clock full-size patterns.

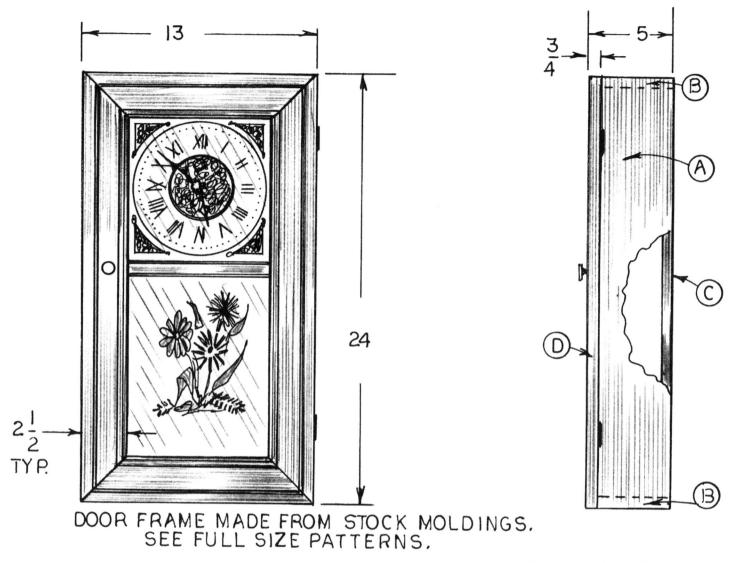

DOOR FRAME MADE FROM STOCK MOLDINGS.
SEE FULL SIZE PATTERNS.

Ogee clock front and side views.

3. Make a dial frame or cleat set and secure this frame to Parts A, ½" back from the front edges. Make a decorative glass panel by reverse painting or covering a glass with a selected decal. Install this panel in the door bottom opening. Install a clear glass panel in the door top opening. Secure with glazier's points or thin wood strips.

4. Set and fill all nailheads. Sand entire reproduction smooth. Stain or paint to a color of choice. Cover with several coats of lacquer or similar finish. Install the movement and the dial. Reinstall the door to Part A. (See Appendix under *Finishing* for suggestions.)

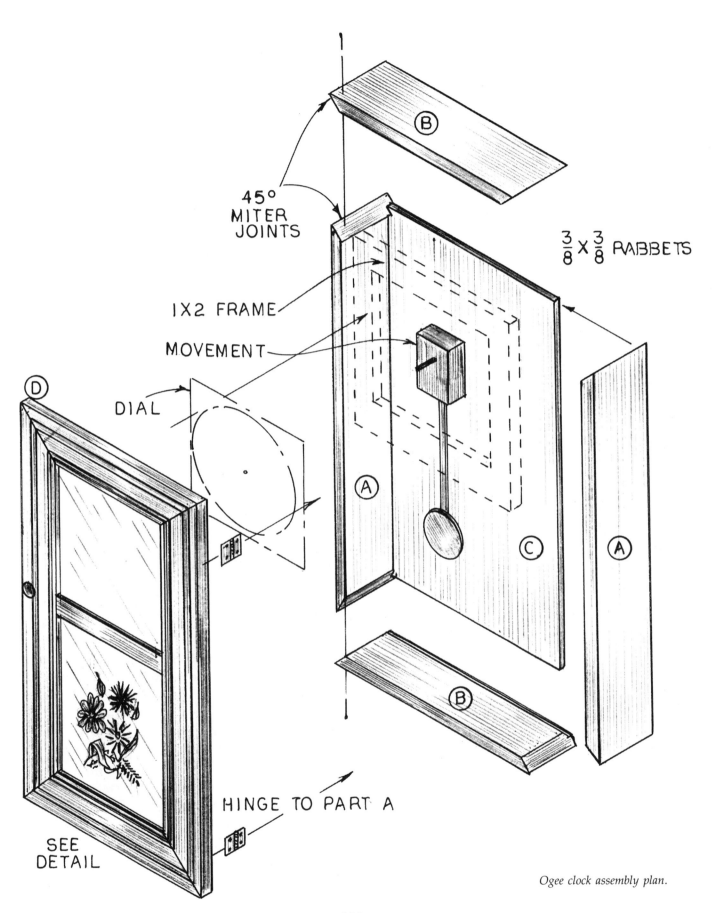

45°
MITER
JOINTS

$\frac{3}{8}$ X $\frac{3}{8}$ RABBETS

1X2 FRAME

MOVEMENT

DIAL

Ⓓ

Ⓑ

Ⓐ

Ⓒ

Ⓐ

Ⓑ

HINGE TO PART A

SEE
DETAIL

Ogee clock assembly plan.

Long-drop Regulator with Broken Pediment (Circa late 1800s)

In the very late 1800s and early 1900s, several hundred different styles of clocks were made that became known as "Regulators" because of their extreme accuracy. The "Schoolhouse" and "Office Regulator" were only two of the many different styles and designs of this clock series.

The following reproduction was developed from several different models and employs the broken arch pediment often found in some tall case clocks.

Material List

Part		Number	Size
A	Side	2	5″ x 27⅝″ x ¾″
B	Base	1	6¾″ x 15″ x ¾″
C	Top	1	5″ x 12″ x ¾″
D	Back	1	11¼″ x 27⅝″ x ⅜″
E	Fascia	1	5″ x 13½″ x ¾″
E1	Ends	2	3″ x 5¾″ x ¾″
F	Roof	2	3″ x 6½″ x ¾″
G	Door	1	12″ x 26″ x ¾″

Wood or brass finial, 1¾″ dia. x 3½″ typical
8″ dia. dial of choice
Movement of choice with pendulum
Lyre or decorative pendulum

CONSTRUCTION

1. Lay out and cut Parts A, B, C, and D to shape and size. Cut a ⅜″ x ⅜″ rabbet on the rear inside edges of Parts A. Cut a molded edge on the front and ends of Part B. Nail or screw Parts B and C into Parts A. Nail Part D into the rabbets made in Parts A.

2. Lay out and cut Parts E, E1, and F to suggested shape and size. (See full-size patterns for suggestions.) Make 45° miter cuts on Parts E and E1. Part E is secured to Part C with nails or screws. Parts E1 are secured to Parts A and E with nails and/or screws. Nail Parts F to the pediment peaks, on Parts E. Install the finial in the center of Part E.

3. Make a door unit to fit the opening. Use 2″ wide stile and bottom rail, and a 6″ wide top rail. Employ dowel, butt, spline, or half-lap joinery. The top rail (6″) is cut with one half of an 8″ diameter circle to match the dial size and shape..With a router, cut a molded edge on the inside door edges. With a rabbet bit, cut a glass

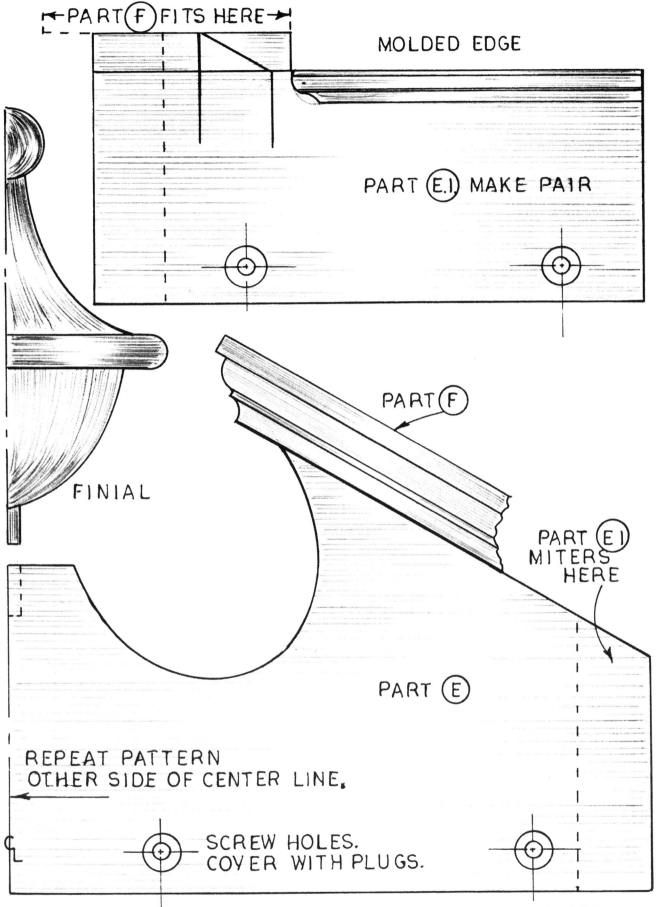

PART F FITS HERE

MOLDED EDGE

PART E.1 MAKE PAIR

FINIAL

PART F

PART E1 MITERS HERE

PART E

REPEAT PATTERN
OTHER SIDE OF CENTER LINE.

SCREW HOLES.
COVER WITH PLUGS.

Long drop full-size patterns.

103

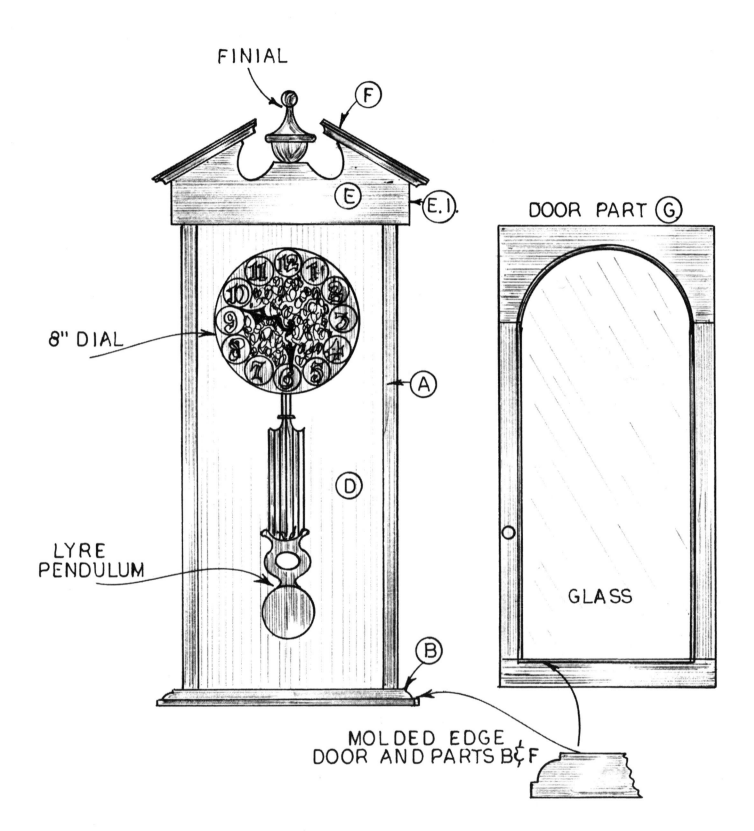

FINIAL

F

E   E.I.

DOOR PART G

8" DIAL

A

D

GLASS

LYRE
PENDULUM

B

MOLDED EDGE
DOOR AND PARTS B&F

Long drop front and side views.

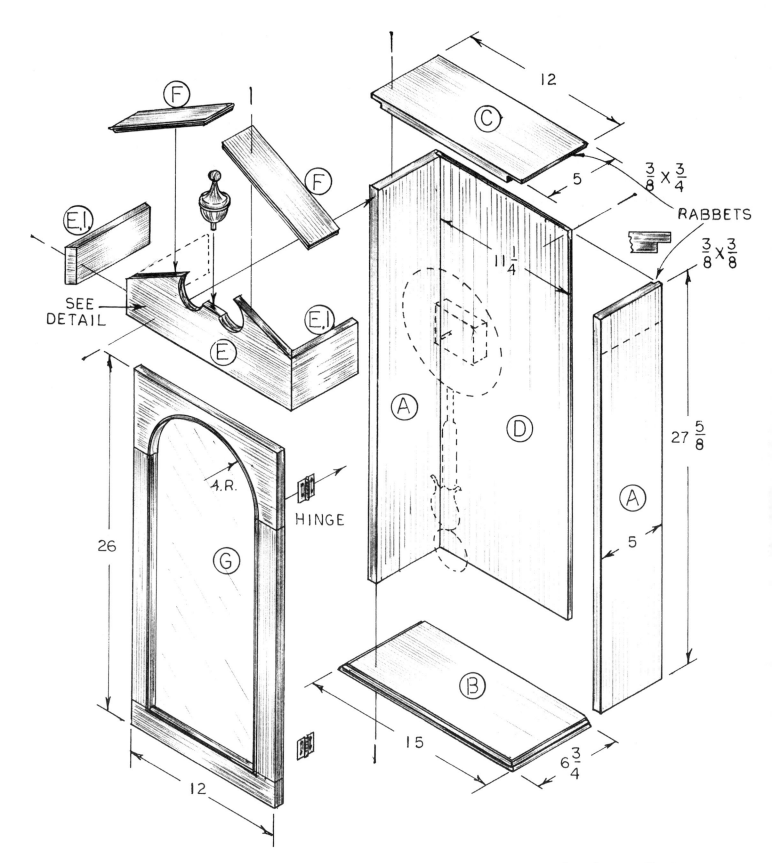

F

F

C

12

E,I

3/8 × 3/4

5

RABBETS

3/8 × 3/8

11 1/4

SEE
DETAIL

E

E,I

A

D

27 5/8

A

HINGE

4.R.

G

26

A

5

B

12

15

6 3/4

Long drop assembly plan.

rabbet on the rear inside edges. Cut the glass to fit into the rabbets and secure with glazier's points or thin wood strips. Secure the door to the right-hand Part A with 1″ x 2″ brass butt hinges. Install a door pull and catch.

4. Remove door and glass. Set and fill all nailheads and cover screwheads with plugs. Sand entire reproduction smooth. Stain or paint to a color of choice. (See Appendix under *Finishing* for suggestions.) Cover with several coats of lacquer or similar finish.

5. Install the movement of choice centered in the arch of the top door rail. Install this round dial so that the doorframe and arch create a frame. Install the movement and the pendulum. A brass beat plaque may be installed under the pendulum center for added authentic finishing. The clock may be hung on a wall or placed upon the wall shelf designed for supporting such wall pieces.

Tall Regulator
(Railroad Regulator)
(Circa late 1800s)

The Tall Regulator was used in railroad stations and was widely known for its high degree of accuracy, hence the name "Regulator." It was often said that if the trains ran as well as the regulator clock, nobody would ever be late. Around 1800 almost every store, railway station, office, and business had one of these clocks.

The following reproduction was developed from antique pieces and incorporates the best-known styles and designs of such timepieces.

Material List

Part	Number	Size
A Sides	2	4″ x 24″ x ¾″
B Base	1	6″ x 15″ x ¾″
C Top	1	6½″ x 15″ x ¾″
D Back	1	9¾″ x 24¾″ x ⅜″
E Fascia	1	3″ x 10½″ x ¾″
F Dentil mold	1	2″ x 11½″ x ⅜″
	2	2″ x 6¾″ x ⅜″
G Molding	1	1¼″ x 13½″ x ¾″
	2	1¼″ x 6¾″ x ¾″
H Cleats	2	2″ x 12″ x ¾″
	2	2″ x 5″ x ¾″
I Door	1	10½″ x 21″ x ¾″

7⅞″ (200mm) square dial
Movement of choice with pendulum
8″ x 9″ stained-glass panel (optional)
8½″ x 8½″ clear glass panel
"Regulator" decal (optional)
Gold stripes decal (optional)

CONSTRUCTION

1. Lay out and cut Parts A, B, C, and D to suggested shape and size. Cut a ⅜″ x ⅜″ rabbet in the rear inside edges of Parts A. Cut a ⅜″ x ⅜″ blind rabbet in Parts B and C. Drill screw pilot holes into Parts B and C. Screw Parts B and C into Parts A to form a box. Nail Part D into the rabbets in the Parts A, B, C assembly.

2. Lay out and cut the fascia—Parts E, F, and G—to shape and size. Make a dentil trim, and sand smooth. Nail Parts F and G with 45° miter joints to Parts E and A just under the joint of Part C. Cut shop-made (or purchased) moldings, Parts G, using 45° mitered corners, and nail these moldings on top of the dentil trim (Parts F) and butting Part C.

3. Make a dial frame, Parts H, using 2″ wide stock. Screw the finish frame to the inside of Parts A, ½″ back from the front edges.

4. Decide the type of door you wish to use: the painted regulator style or the stained-glass design. (See patterns for door styles.) Make a doorframe using 1½″-wide rails and stiles. Cut a glass rabbet into the rear inside edges of the door parts. Cut a molded edge on the outside edges of the door. Secure the door to the right-hand Part A using 1½″ x 1½″ brass butt hinges. Install a door catch and pull. Insert the selected

Oak long drop clock. Author's collection.

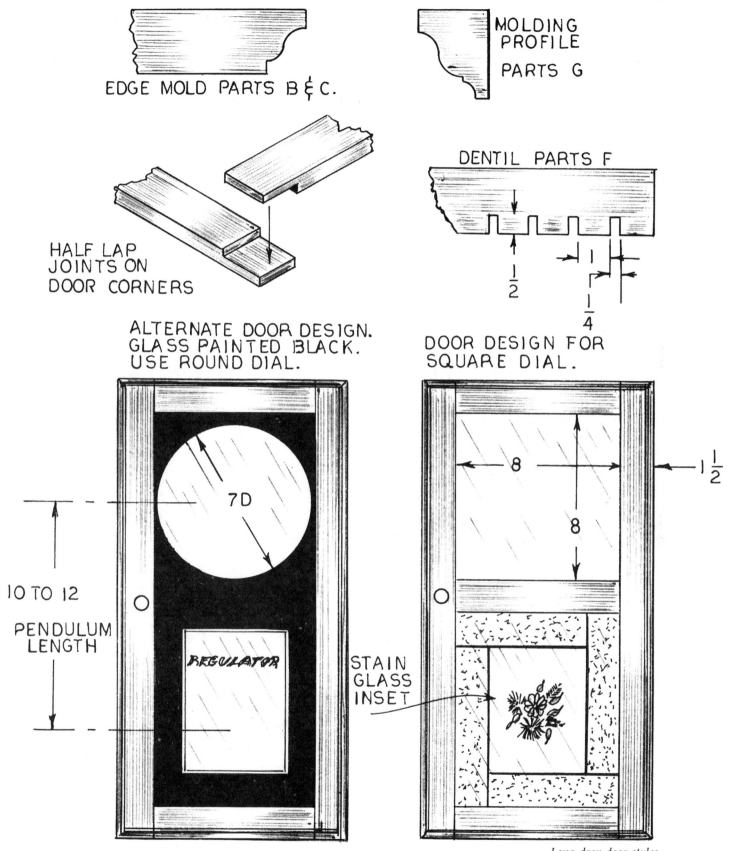

EDGE MOLD PARTS B & C.

MOLDING PROFILE PARTS G

HALF LAP JOINTS ON DOOR CORNERS

DENTIL PARTS F

$\frac{1}{2}$

$\frac{1}{4}$

ALTERNATE DOOR DESIGN. GLASS PAINTED BLACK. USE ROUND DIAL.

DOOR DESIGN FOR SQUARE DIAL.

7D

8

8

$1\frac{1}{2}$

10 TO 12

PENDULUM LENGTH

REGULATOR

STAIN GLASS INSET

Long drop door styles.

109

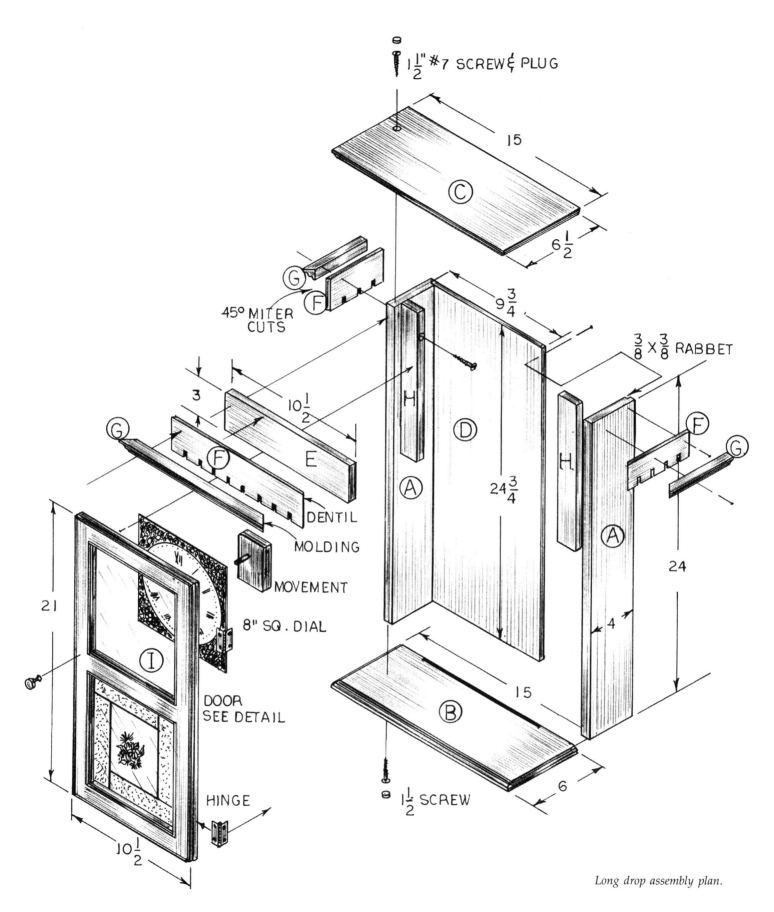

1½" #7 SCREW & PLUG

15

6½

45° MITER CUTS

3

10½

9¾

⅜ X ⅜ RABBET

E

DENTIL MOLDING

MOVEMENT

8" SQ. DIAL

24¾

24

4

15

21

I

DOOR SEE DETAIL

HINGE

10½

B

1½ SCREW

6

Long drop assembly plan.

110

glass into the rabbet and secure with glazier's points or thin wood strips.

5. Set and fill all nailheads. Cover all screwheads with plugs. Sand entire reproduction smooth. Stain to a color of choice. (See Appendix for suggestions on finishing.) Cover with several coats of lacquer or similar finish.

6. Install the movement of choice in the case. Nail or screw blocks may be required. Install the clock dial over the movement, and center it within the frame made by the glass in the door. The clock may be hung on a wall or supported by using the standard clock shelf shown elsewhere in this book.

Vienna Regulator-style Clock (Circa mid-1800s)

The "Crown"- or "Vienna"-style regulator clock was designed from the standard Victorian clock that often became known as the "European Regulator" throughout the 19th century. Often, the later-period Victorian clocks contained overembellished carvings, turnings, and moldings.

The following reproduction was designed with almost simplistic lines in keeping with the classical form used throughout this book.

Material List

Part		Number	Size
A	Sides	2	4″ x 26″ x ¾″
B	Back	1	10½″ x 26″ x ⅜″
C	Top	1	4″ x 11″ x ¾″
D	Base	1	6″ x 13″ x ¾″
E	Fascia	1	6″ x 11″ x ¾″
		2	2″ x 6″ x ¾″
F	Crown molding	1	¾″ x ¾″ x 13″
		2	¾″ x ¾″ x 5″
G	Bead molding	1	¾″ x ⅝″ x 13″
		2	¾″ x ⅝″ x 5″
H	Door	1	11″ x 23⅓″ x ¾″

Movement of choice, 16″ pendulum
8″ dia. dial of choice
Brass beat plaque
Glass panel, 3½″ x 20½″

CONSTRUCTION

1. Lay out and cut Parts A, B, C, and D to shape and size. Cut a ⅜″ x ⅜″ rabbet on the rear inside edges of Parts A. Cut a ⅜″ x ¾″ rabbet on the ends of Part C. Cut a molded edge on the front and ends of Part D. Nail Part C into Parts A. Nail Part B into the rabbets in Parts A. Nail or screw Part D up into Parts A.

2. Lay out the crown fascia, Part E, and the crown molding, Parts F. (See full-size patterns for designs. See instructions for making swan-neck molding for suggested techniques.) *Note: 45° miter joints are needed for Parts F.* Glue the crown molding, Part F, to the crown fascia, Part E. Screw Part E assembly to Parts A and C. Make the side moldings, Parts F, and secure them to Parts A and the front crown molding. Cut the small bead moldings, Parts G, to size and, using 45° miter joints, attach them to Parts A and E as noted in the full-size patterns.

3. Make a door, Part H, by using 1½″ side stiles and bottom rail and a half-round 5″ top rail. (See arch design in orthographic drawing.) Use butt, dowel, spline, or half-lap joinery for construction. Cut a glass rabbet on the rear inside edges of the door. Cut a molded bead

Vienna-style regulator.

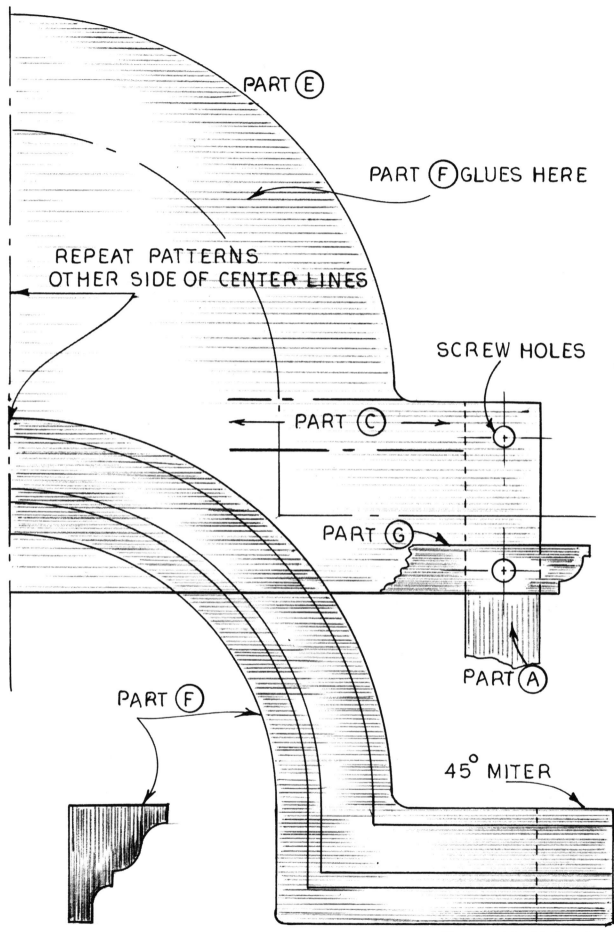

PART (E)

PART (F) GLUES HERE

REPEAT PATTERNS
OTHER SIDE OF CENTER LINES

SCREW HOLES

PART (C)

PART (G)

PART (A)

PART (F)

45° MITER

Vienna regulator full-size patterns.

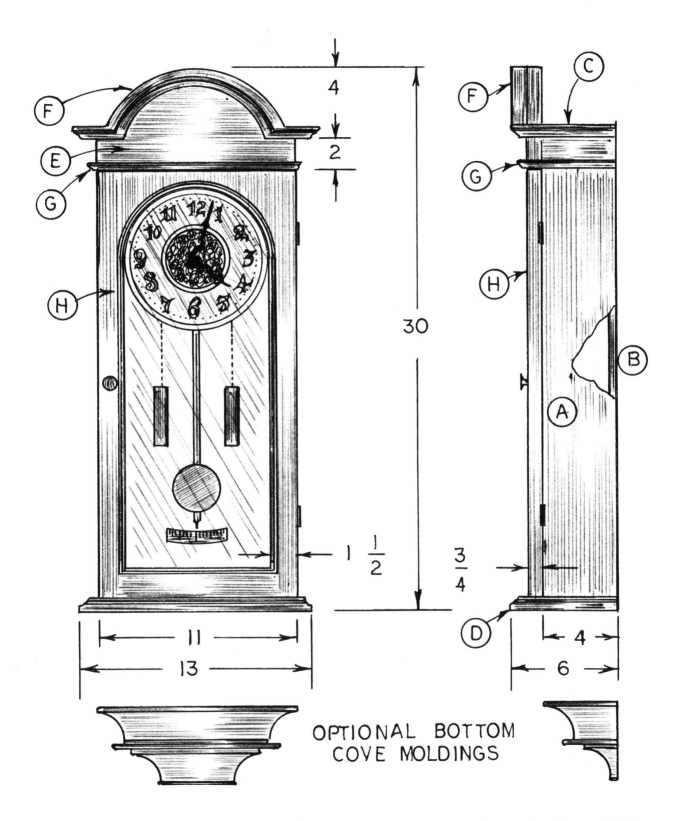

OPTIONAL BOTTOM
COVE MOLDINGS

Vienna regulator front and side views.

115

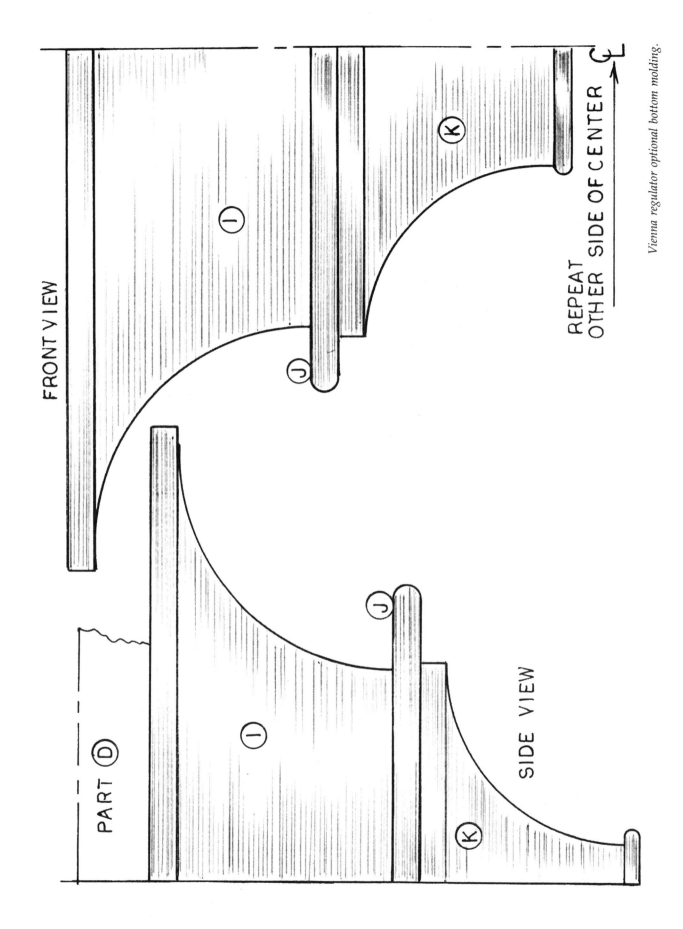

FRONT VIEW

PART D

SIDE VIEW

REPEAT OTHER SIDE OF CENTER

Vienna regulator optional bottom molding.

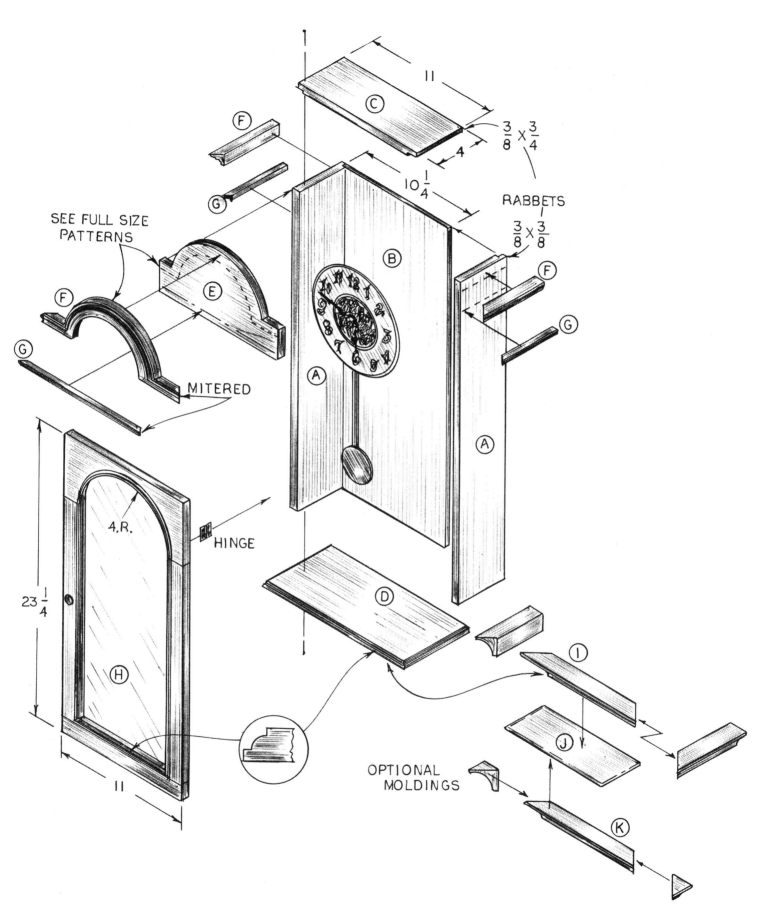

11

C

$\frac{3}{8} \times \frac{3}{4}$

4

$10\frac{1}{4}$

RABBETS

$\frac{3}{8} \times \frac{3}{8}$

F

G

SEE FULL SIZE
PATTERNS

F

E

B

F

G

G

A

A

MITERED

D

I

4,R.

HINGE

J

23$\frac{1}{4}$

H

OPTIONAL
MOLDINGS

K

11

Vienna regulator assembly plan.

on the outside inner edges of the door. Attach the finished door to Part A using 1″ x 1½″ brass butt hinges. Attach a door catch and small brass pull.

4. Set and fill all nailheads. Cover all screwheads with plugs. Sand entire reproduction smooth. Stain to a color of choice. Cover with several coats of lacquer or similar finish.

5. Install the glass panel, Part I, in the doorframe using glazier's points or thin wood strips. Mount the movement of choice using glue or screw blocks. Mount the dial centered in the arched crown of the doorframe opening. Install the pendulum and beat plaque if desired. *Note: This clock may be hung on a wall, but it looks best if used with the universal clock shelf.*

Schoolhouse Regulator-style (Circa late 1800s)

This clock received its name because it was widely used in classrooms and other public buildings in the late 1800s. The "Schoolhouse Regulator" is kin to all the other regulator-style clocks used throughout this time period.

The following reproduction was developed along the classical lines of antique pieces and is offered with a stained-glass bottom door panel if preferred to the black painted oval on the original clocks. (Check construction methods for ansonial-style clock for suggestions.)

Material List

Part	Number	Size
A Sides	2	4" x 13¼" x ¾"
B End	2	4" x 4½" x ¾"
C Bottom	1	4" x 3" x ¾"
D Back	1	8¼" x 15¼" x ⅜"
E Top	1	4" x 9" x ¾"
F Plaque	1	12" x 12" x ¾"
G Molding	8	6" x ¾" x ¾"
H Door	1	7" x 9" x ¾"

10" dia. dial, with or without calendar ring
Movement of choice with 8" pendulum
Glass panel, 7½" x 4½" (stained glass optional)

CONSTRUCTION

1. Lay out and cut Parts A, B, C, D, and E to shape and size. (See full-size patterns for suggestions.) Cut a ⅜" x ⅜" rabbet on the rear inside edges of Parts A, B, C, and D. Cut a ⅜" x ¾" rabbet on both ends of Part E. *Note: Use 22½° angle cuts for miters on Parts A, B, and C.* With spline, dowel, or butt joinery, join Parts A, B, and C together to form the base angle shown in full-size patterns. Nail Part E to Parts A. Nail Part D into the rabbets in Parts A, B, C, and E.

2. Lay out and cut the front plaque and moldings if used. (See full-size patterns. For optional methods of making the octagon front plaque see construction methods for ansonial-style clock.) *Note: The bottom of Part F is not cut in a pure octagon, but made square at the width of 9" or the width of the Parts A, B, C, D, and E assembly. The moldings, Parts G, however, are secured on the pure octagon angles.* Make Part F in method chosen. Cut a movement recess or seat hole in Part F.

Cherry schoolhouse regulator clock.

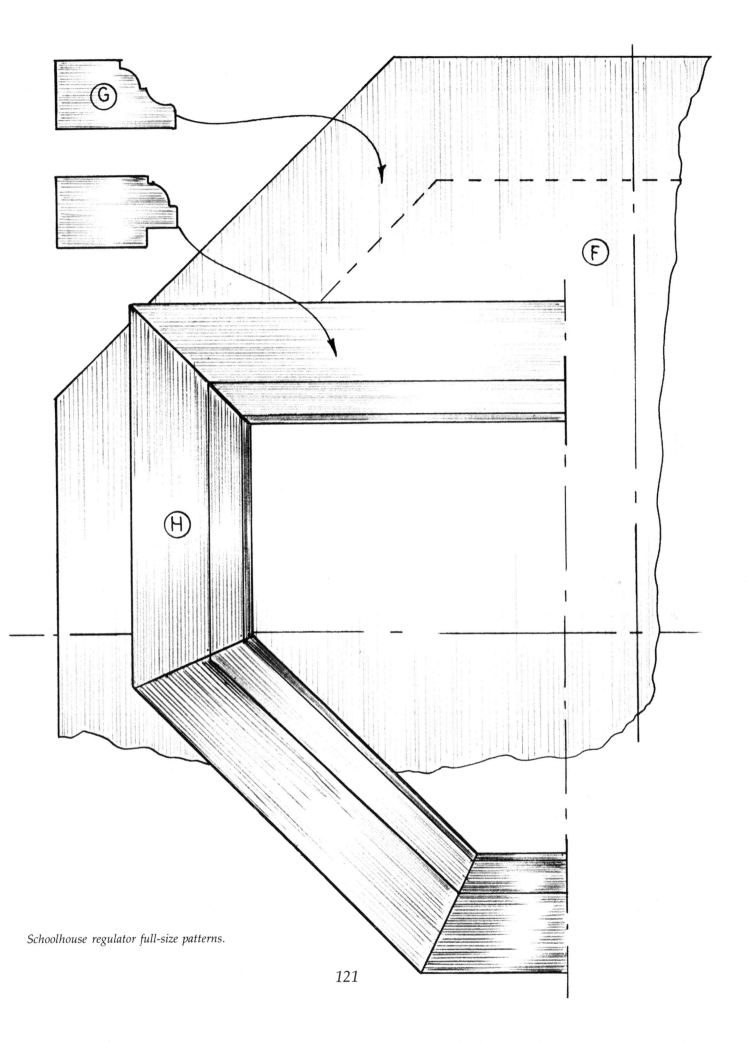

Schoolhouse regulator full-size patterns.

121

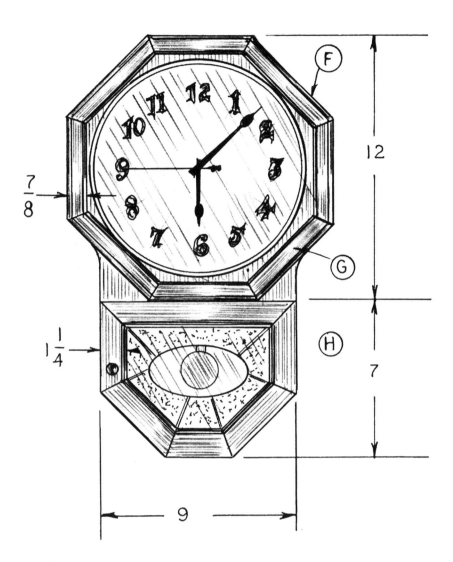

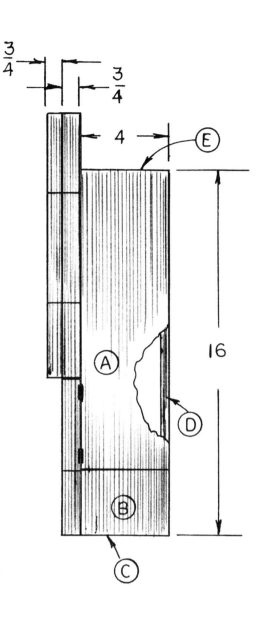

Schoolhouse regulator front and side views.

With dowel pins, screws, or nails, secure Part F to Parts A and D. Glue and nail Parts G to Part F if used. These add-on moldings employ 22½° miter cuts.

3. Make a door unit to match the angles and shapes of the lower box formed by Parts A, B, and C. Use 1¼" wide rails and stiles. Cut a glass rabbet on the rear inside edges of the finished door. Attach the door to the right-hand Part A with 1" x 1" brass butt hinges. Install a catch and door pull. Install a painted or clear glass panel in the door opening. *Note: A stained-glass unit made with an oval center shape for pendulum viewing may be used if preferred.* Secure the chosen glass in the rabbet with glazier's points or thin wood stops.

4. Set and fill all nailheads. Cover all screwheads with plugs. Sand smooth. Stain to a color of choice. Cover with several coats of lacquer or similar finish. (See Appendix under *Finishing* for suggestions.) Install chosen dial/bezel and movement.

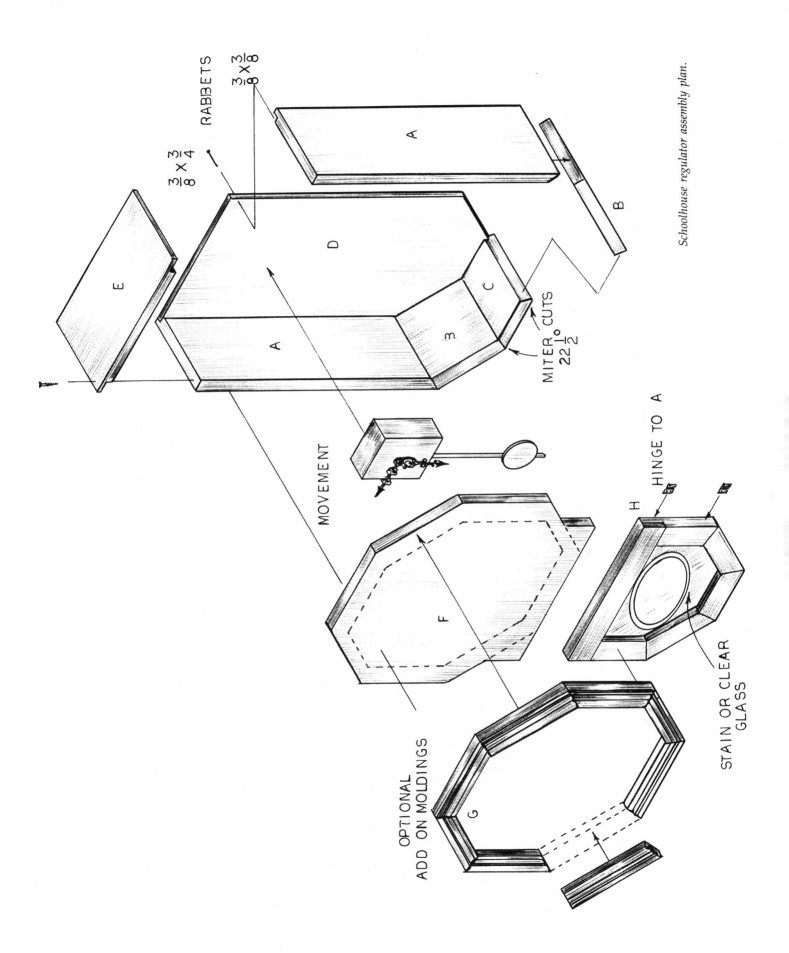

RABBETS

$\frac{3}{8} \times \frac{3}{8}$

$\frac{3}{8} \times \frac{3}{4}$

A

B

E

D

A

C

B

MITER CUTS
$22\frac{1}{2}°$

MOVEMENT

F

OPTIONAL
ADD ON MOLDINGS

G

H

HINGE TO A

STAIN OR CLEAR
GLASS

Schoolhouse regulator assembly plan.

Schoolhouse-style short-drop regulator clock. Heritage Clock Co., Lexington, North Carolina.

Ansonial-style Octagon Long Drop (Circa mid-1800s)

The "Octagon Long Drop" is a sister to the schoolhouse clock, with a few minor changes. The pendulum case is much longer, and it is finished in a point rather than a half-octagon like the schoolhouse-type clock. Several hundred different variations of this style clock were made, and the Seth Thomas and Ansonial units are now priceless collector's items. (See drawing for suggestion for construction methods.)

Material List

Part	Number	Size
A Sides	2	4″ x 25″ x ¾″
B Base	2	4″ x 6″ x ¾″
C Back	1	8¼″ x 30″ x ⅜″
D Top	1	4¾″ x 10″ x ¾″
E Backer	1	10″ x 12″ x ¾″
F Door	1	10″ x 18″ x ¾″
G Front	1	16″ x 16″ x ¾″

12″ dia. dial/bezel combination

Movement of choice with 16″ pendulum

Glass panel, 9″ x 16½″

"Regulator" and gold stripe decals if desired

CONSTRUCTION

1. Lay out and cut Parts A and B to size and shape. Cut a ⅜″ x ⅜″ rabbet on the rear inside edges of Parts A, B, and D. Make 22½° miter cuts on the bottom and join parts A and B. Nail or screw Part D into Parts A. Nail Part C into the rabbets on Part A, B, and D.

2. Lay out and cut Part E to shape and size. Screw or nail Part E to Parts A and D. Lay out the octagon front panel, Part G. (This piece may be made by any one of several different methods; see drawing for suggestions.) Screw the finished Part G to Part E. The screws should be placed so that the clock dial/bezel will cover the heads. A movement housing or seat hole should be cut through Parts E and G.

3. Make a door unit using 1½″ framing members; spline, dowel, or half-lap joinery is suggested. The door should match the sizes and angle formed by the joining of Parts A and B. It is suggested that the door unit be made

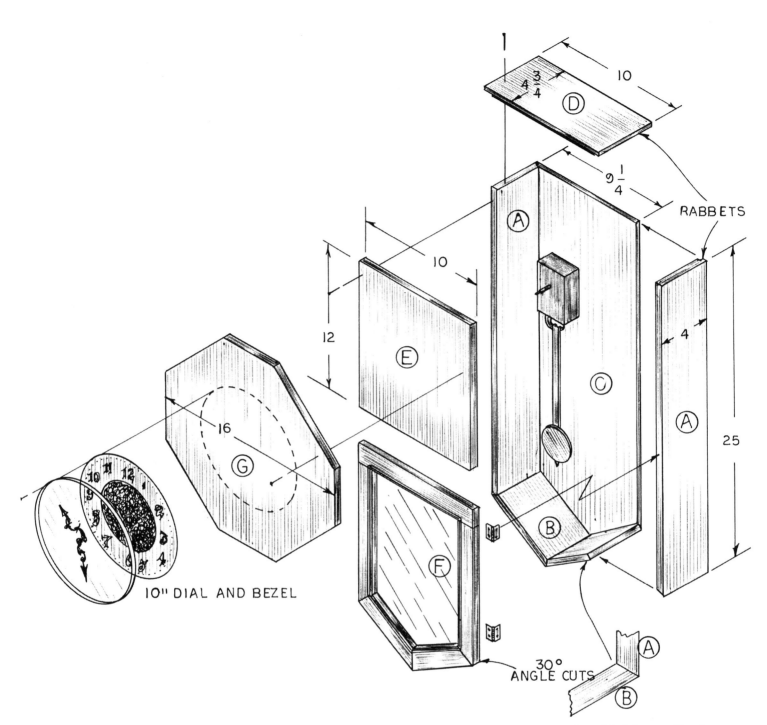

10" DIAL AND BEZEL

Ansonial-style assembly plan.

slightly larger than needed and sanded down to final size. Cut a glass rabbet on the rear inside edges of the door. Secure the glass panel in the rabbets using glazier's points or thin wood stops.

4. Set and fill all nailheads. Cover all exposed screwheads with plugs. Sand entire reproduction smooth. Stain or paint to a color of choice.

Cover with several coats of lacquer or similar finish. (See Appendix under *Finishing* for suggestions.) Install the movement to the bezel dial. Install the assembly to the clock plaque front. Install the pendulum. A "Regulator" decal and gold stripe decals may be applied to the door glass if desired. Check clock suppliers for possible combinations.

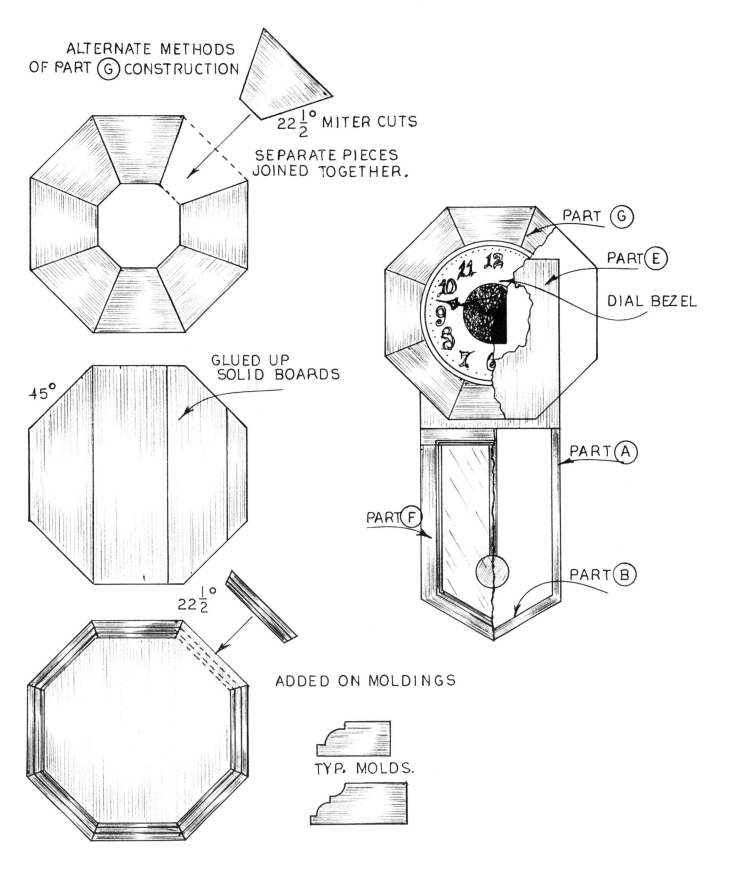

ALTERNATE METHODS OF PART Ⓖ CONSTRUCTION

$22\frac{1}{2}°$ MITER CUTS

SEPARATE PIECES JOINED TOGETHER.

$45°$

GLUED UP SOLID BOARDS

$22\frac{1}{2}°$

ADDED ON MOLDINGS

TYP. MOLDS.

PART Ⓖ

PART Ⓔ

DIAL BEZEL

PART Ⓐ

PART Ⓕ

PART Ⓑ

Ansonial-style construction methods.

127

Courthouse Hexagon Clock
(Circa late 1800s)

I named this regulator-style clock the "Courthouse Hexagon" because that is where I first saw it. It is a variation of the regular octagon-style regulator, designed in many variations in the late 1800s and early 1900s.

Material List

Part	Number	Size
A Sides	2	3½″ x 21¼″ x ¾″
B Base	2	3½″ x 5″ x ¾″
C Top	1	3½″ x 8″ x ¾″
D Back	1	7¼″ x 22¾″ x ⅜″
E Plaque	1	12″ x 14″ x ¾″
F Molding	6	¾″ x ⅞″ x 7¼″
G Door	1	8″ x 12½″ x ¾″

8″ to 9½″ dia. dial/bezel combination
Movement of choice with 16″ pendulum
Glass panel, 6½″ x 9½″

Note: The plaque front, Part E, is made of a solid block with add-on moldings cut on 30° miters. (See construction methods for ansonial-style clock for other suggestions on this construction.)

CONSTRUCTION

1. Lay out and cut Parts A, B, and C to shape and size. Cut a ⅜″ x ⅜″ rabbet on the rear inside edges of each part. Cut a ⅜″ x ¾″ rabbet on both ends of Part C. *Note: 30° angle cuts on Parts A and B.* Glue, nail, or spline-join Parts A to Parts B. Nail Part C into Parts A. Cut Part D to size and nail it into the rabbets cut into Parts A, B, and C.

2. Lay out the hexagon shape on Part E. Cut the moldings, Parts F, to size using 30° miters. Glue and nail Parts F to Part E. Cut a movement seat or relief access hole in the center of Part E. Dowel-pin, nail, or screw the finished Part E to Parts A and C.

3. Make a door to match the angles and size of the bottom assembly made up of Parts A and B. Cut a glass rabbet into the rear inside edges of this door. Hinge the door to the right-hand Part A using 1″ x 1″ brass butt hinges. Install

Courthouse regulator hexagon, made from pine.

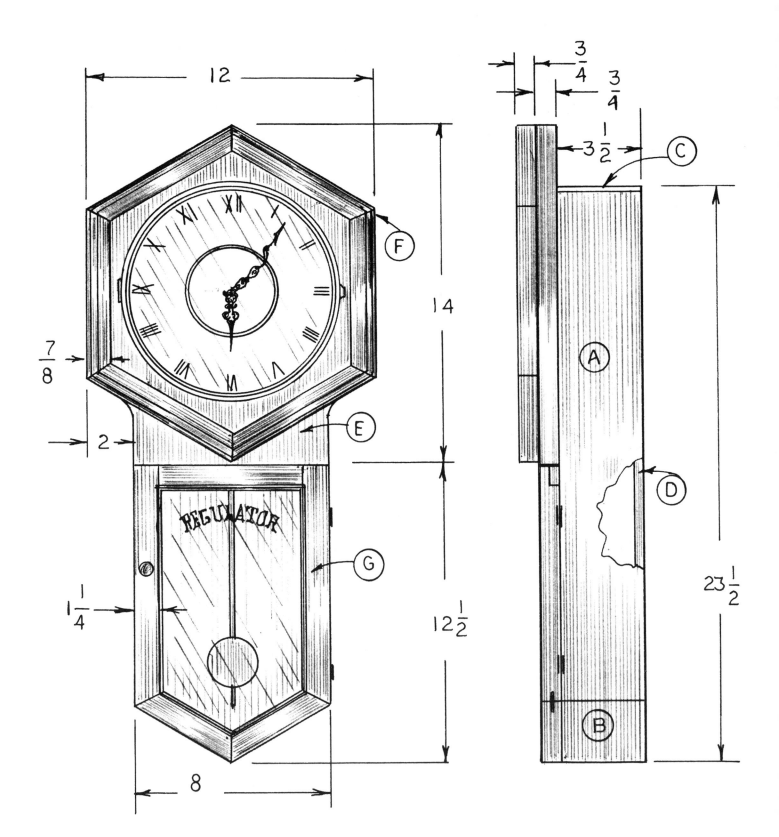

Courthouse hexagon front and side views.

130

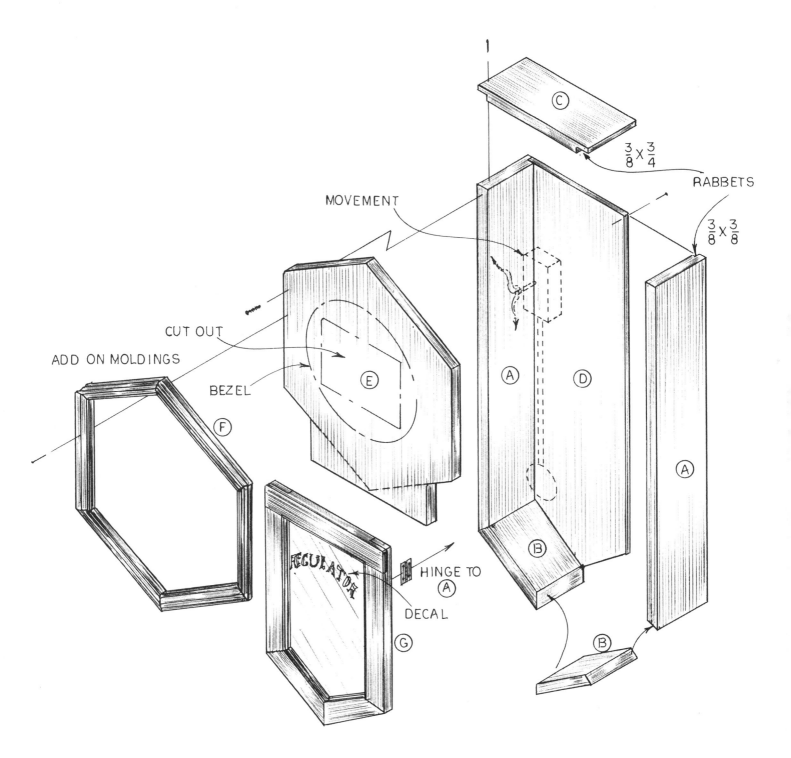

MOVEMENT

CUT OUT

ADD ON MOLDINGS

BEZEL

REGULATOR

HINGE TO
Ⓐ

DECAL

$\frac{3}{8}$ X $\frac{3}{4}$

RABBETS

$\frac{3}{8}$ X $\frac{3}{8}$

Ⓐ Ⓑ Ⓒ Ⓓ Ⓔ Ⓕ Ⓖ

Courthouse hexagon assembly plan.

131

the glass in the glass rabbet using glazier's points or thin wood stops. *Note: A "Regulator" and gold stripe decal may be installed on the glass panel if desired. Stained glass may also be used.*

4. Set and fill all nailheads. Cover all screwheads with plugs. Sand entire reproduction smooth. Stain or paint to a color of choice. (See Appendix under *Finishing* for suggestions.) Cover with several coats of lacquer or similar finish. Secure the movement to the dial using the threaded nut and hand shaft. Install the dial/bezel unit to the front of Part E. Install the pendulum. Install hanging hook on the top of Part C center.

Round Regulator-style (Circa mid-1800s)

The following clock was developed in part from an original Seth Thomas, Number Two Regulator. It has the round ring surrounding the dial, and while the original clock had a square bottom, this offering continues the round theme to include the bottom and the lower door rail.

Material List

Part	Number	Size
A Sides	2	3″ x 16″ x ¾″
B Bottom	½	9″ dia. circle x ¾″

The 9″ dia. circle is turned on a lathe and then cut in half to form the case bottom.

C Back	1	8¼″ x 20½″ x ⅜″
D Top	1	3¾″ x 9″ x ¾″
E Front	1	7″ x 9″ x ¾″
F Door	1	9″ x 13½″ x ¾″
G Ring	1	12″ dia. x 1¼″

Bezel/dial combination, 8″–10″ dia.
Movement of choice with pendulum
Door glass panel, 6″ x 10½″

CONSTRUCTION

1. Lay out and cut Parts A, C, and D to shape and size. Lathe-turn Part B as a bowl with a ¾″ sidewall thickness. Both the interior and exterior areas should be well sanded while the piece is still on the lathe. Cut this bowl forming Part B in half. Make a saw blade spline dado in Parts A and B, as shown in assembly drawing. With a hardwood spline, glue Parts A and B together. Nail Part D to the top of Parts A. With a router and rabbet bit, cut a ⅜″ x ⅜″ rabbet on the back rear inside edges of Parts A, B, and D. Nail Part C into these rabbets. Nail or screw Part E to Parts A and D.

2. Make a door by turning a circle 9″ in diameter with sidewall widths of 1⅜″ and a thickness of ¾″. Cut this circle in half. This circle should match the bowl-like half-circle, Part B. It is suggested that this door circle be made slightly larger and sanded into final shape. Cut

133

Round regulator, made from pine.

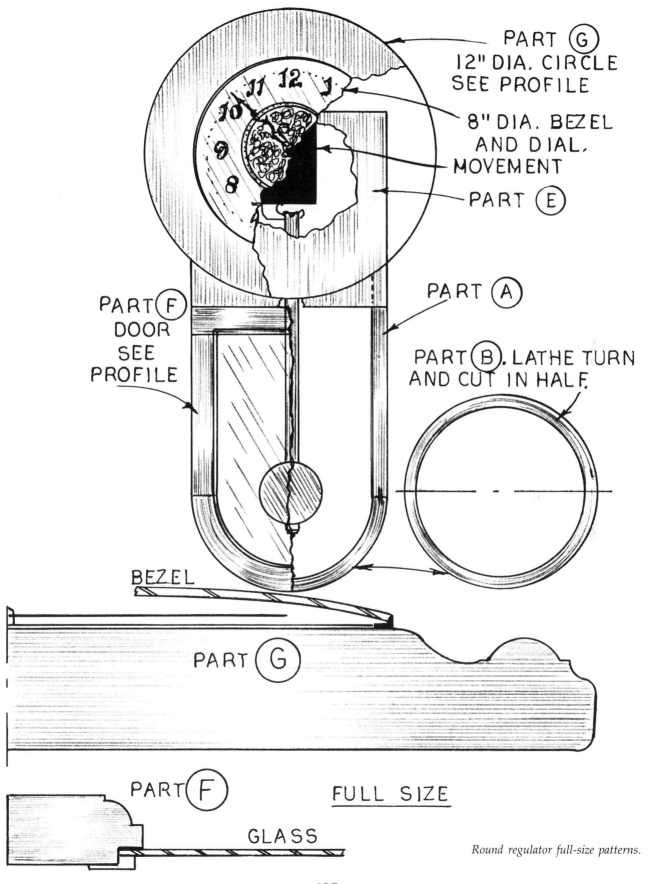

PART Ⓖ
12" DIA. CIRCLE
SEE PROFILE

8" DIA. BEZEL
AND DIAL,
MOVEMENT

PART Ⓔ

PART Ⓕ
DOOR
SEE
PROFILE

PART Ⓐ

PART Ⓑ. LATHE TURN
AND CUT IN HALF.

BEZEL

PART Ⓖ

PART Ⓕ

FULL SIZE

GLASS

Round regulator full-size patterns.

135

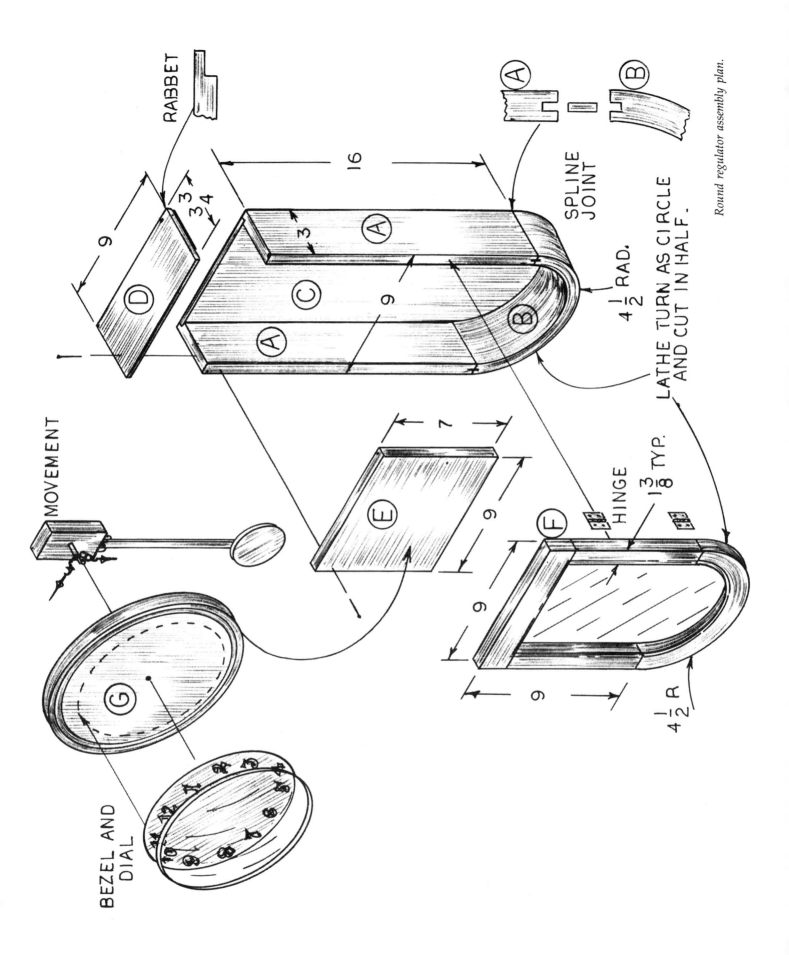

RABBET

SPLINE JOINT

Ⓐ ─ ⓘ ─ Ⓑ

$4\frac{1}{2}$ RAD.

LATHE TURN AS CIRCLE AND CUT IN HALF.

16

9

$3\frac{3}{4}$

3

Ⓐ

Ⓒ

Ⓐ

9

Ⓓ

Ⓑ

7

Ⓔ

9

9

HINGE

$1\frac{3}{8}$ TYP.

Ⓕ

9

9

$4\frac{1}{2}$ R

MOVEMENT

Ⓖ

BEZEL AND DIAL

Round regulator assembly plan.

a spline notch into the ends of this half-circle. Glue a hardwood spline into the half-circle and the door stiles. Glue the door top rail in place. With a router, cut a glass rabbet in the rear inside edges and cut a molded edge on the exterior inside edges. (See detail in full-size patterns.) Secure the door to the right-hand Part A with 1¼" x 1¼" brass butt hinges. Attach a catch and small brass pull.

3. Lathe-turn the round for the ring, Part G. Mark out the location of the bezel frame and turn a seat for the bezel while turning the decorative ring plaque. Cut a movement seat or recess hole into Part G, and a matching hole in Part E. Secure Part G to Part E with screws.

4. Set and fill all nailheads. Cover all exposed screwheads with plugs. Sand entire reproduction smooth. Stain or paint to a color of choice. (See Appendix under *Finishing* for suggestions.) Cover with several coats of lacquer or similar finish. Secure the movement to the dial by means of a threaded nut and the threaded hand shaft. Secure the dial/bezel movement to Part G with small screws or pins. Attach the pendulum. Secure the glass panel in the door with glazier's points or thin wood stops. A decal of black or gold stripes or the trade name "Regulator" may be applied to the glass if desired.

Granddaughter-style Wall Clock (Circa late 1700s)

The "Granddaughter-style" wall clock was designed from the top hood section of a tall case, hall clock popular in Colonial and early American times. This clock incorporates the usual swan-neck pediment, turned columns, a finial, and an ornate dial common to the tall case designs of the late 1700s. This unique clock has been designed as a wall piece using features most often sought in a decorative, as well as functional, clock, yet developed for an area limited in floor space.

Material List

Part		Number	Size
A	Sides	2	4″ x 28½″ x ¾″
B	Back	1	10½″ x 28½″ x ⅜″
C	Top	1	4″ x 11″ x ¾″
D	Fascia	1	4″ x 11″ x ¾″
E	Ledger front	1	1½″ x 15″ x ¾″
F	Side ledgers	2	1½″ x 7″ x ¾″
G	Swan-neck	2	6″ x 4″ x ¾″
H	Side molds	2	1″ x 7″ x ¾″
I	Bottom mold	1	1½″ x 15″ x ¾″
J	Side molds	2	1½″ x 7″ x ¾″
K	Column	1	1¼″ dia. x 12″
L	Door	1	12″ x 11″ x ¾″
M	Finial	1	1¾″ dia. x 3½″

Movement of choice with 12″–16″ pendulum
8″ x 8″ dial, grandmother style
Glass panel, 8½″ x 8½″

CONSTRUCTION

1. Lay out and cut Parts A, B, and C to shape and size. (See full-size patterns for Parts A and B.) Cut a ⅜″ x ¾″ rabbet on the rear inside edges of Parts A. Nail Part B into the rabbets. Cut a ⅜″ x ¾″ rabbet on each end of Part C. Nail Part C into Part A and B.

2. Lay out and cut Part D, E, F, G, and H to shape and size. (See full-size patterns for Parts D, E, F, and G. See instruction for making the swan-neck pediment at the start of this section.) Glue Part G to Part D, using 45° miter joints. Glue and screw Parts H to Parts A. Screw Part D into Parts A and C. Cut a decorative molded edge on Parts E and F. Using 45° miter corners, glue and screw Parts E and F to Parts A and D.

3. Lay out and cut Parts I and J to shape and size. Cut a molded edge on these parts. (See full-size patterns for suggested designs.) Make 45° miter cuts and screw Parts J to Parts A. Screw Part I to Parts A and Parts J. Lathe turn or purchase Part K, the half-columns. Glue one half of the column to each Part A, in between Parts F and J.

4. Make a door of 1¾″ wide rails and stiles using butt, dowel, spline, or half-lap joinery.

Granddaughter-style wall clock, made from pine. Author's collection.

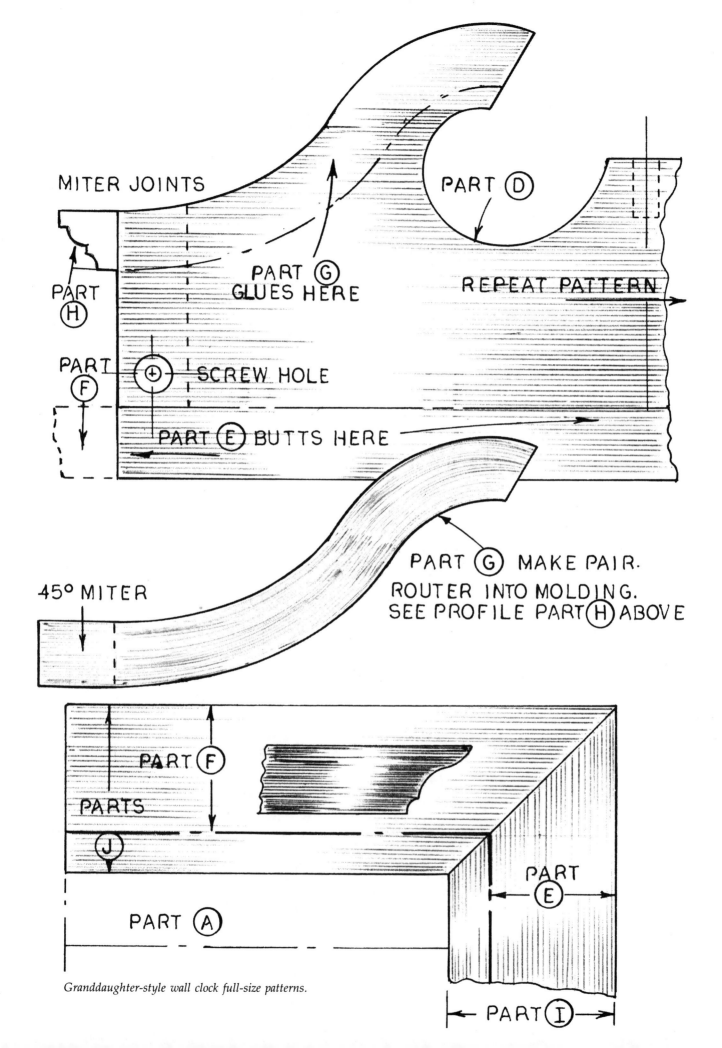

MITER JOINTS

PART ⓓ

REPEAT PATTERN

PART ⓖ
GLUES HERE

PART ⓗ

PART ⓕ

⊕ SCREW HOLE

PART ⓔ BUTTS HERE

45° MITER

PART ⓖ MAKE PAIR.
ROUTER INTO MOLDING.
SEE PROFILE PART ⓗ ABOVE

PART ⓕ

PARTS

ⓙ

PART ⓔ

PART ⓐ

PART ⓘ

Granddaughter-style wall clock full-size patterns.

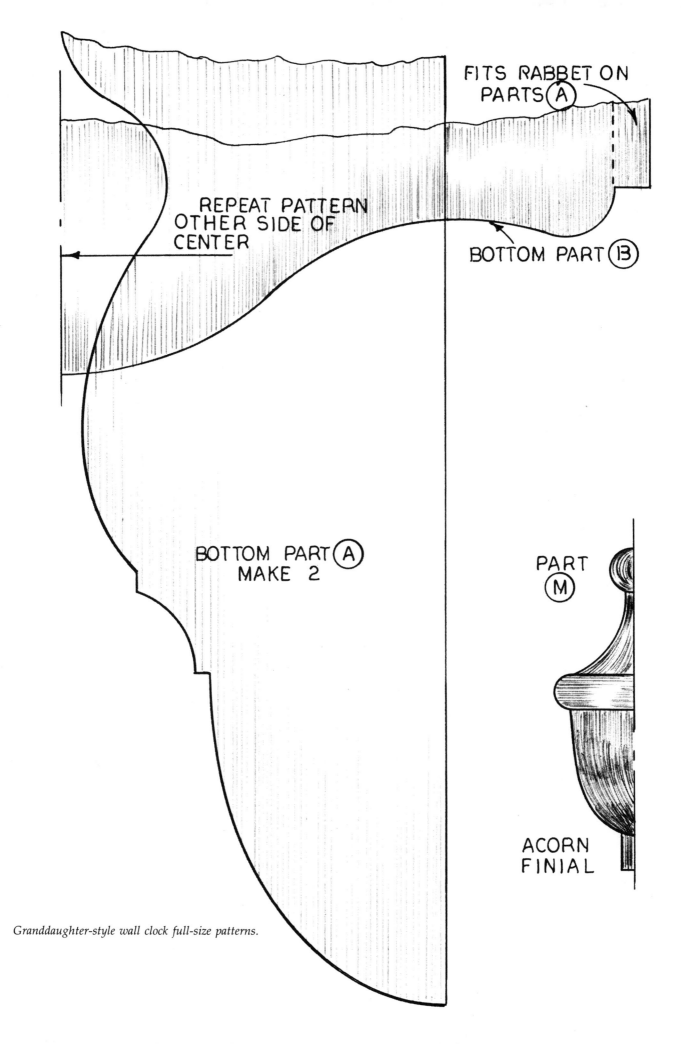

FITS RABBET ON PARTS (A)

REPEAT PATTERN OTHER SIDE OF CENTER

BOTTOM PART (B)

BOTTOM PART (A) MAKE 2

PART (M)

ACORN FINIAL

Granddaughter-style wall clock full-size patterns.

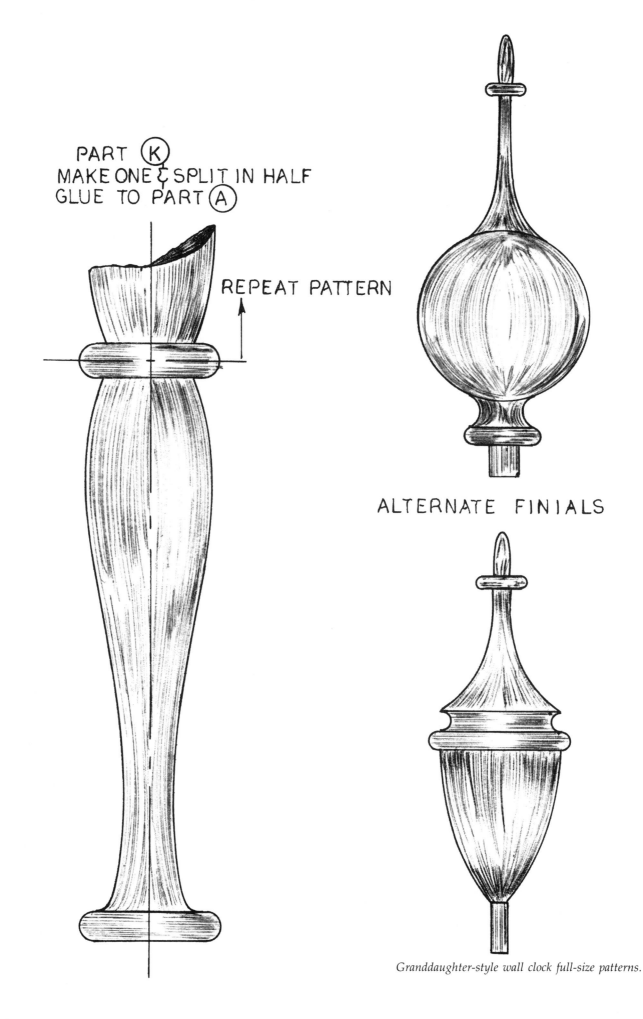

PART Ⓚ
MAKE ONE & SPLIT IN HALF
GLUE TO PART Ⓐ

REPEAT PATTERN

ALTERNATE FINIALS

Granddaughter-style wall clock full-size patterns.

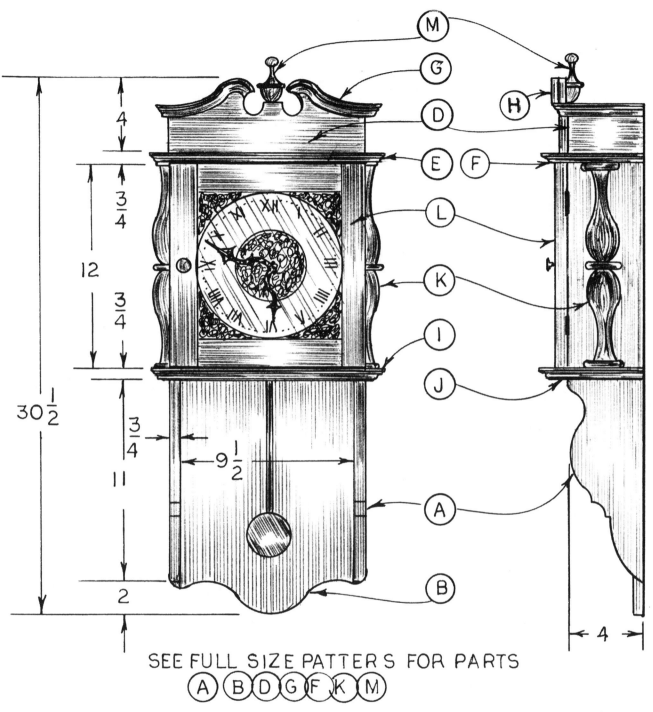

SEE FULL SIZE PATTERNS FOR PARTS
(A) (B) (D) (G) (F) (K) (M)

Granddaughter-style wall clock front and side views.

Cut a glass rabbet on the rear inside edges of the door. Cut a molded design on the outside edge of the door. Install the door to the right-hand Part A using 1″ x 1″ brass butt hinges.

5. Make a dial frame or cleat backer and install it to Parts A, ½″ back from the front edges. Cut a movement relief (access) hole in the solid backer if used. Mount a movement and dial

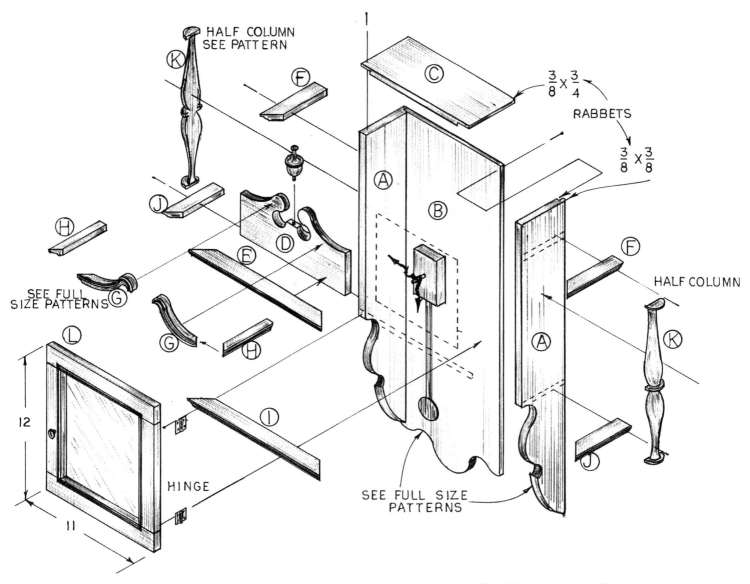

HALF COLUMN
SEE PATTERN

K

F

C

$\frac{3}{8} \times \frac{3}{4}$

RABBETS

$\frac{3}{8} \times \frac{3}{8}$

A

B

J

H

D

E

F

HALF COLUMN

SEE FULL
SIZE PATTERNS

G

G

A

H

K

L

I

J

12

HINGE

SEE FULL SIZE
PATTERNS

11

Granddaughter-style wall clock assembly plan.

centered within the open glass area of the finished door.

6. Set and fill all nailheads. Fill all screwheads with plugs. Sand the entire clock smooth. Stain to a color of choice. Cover with several coats of lacquer or similar finish. (See Appendix under *Finishing* for suggestions.) Remount the dial and movement. Install glass in the door glass rabbets using glazier's points or thin wood stops. Install a door catch and pull.

Shaker Wall Clock (Circa early 1800s)

The following clock was designed from a clock made by Isaac N. Youngs. It is now on display at the Hancock Shaker Village, Hancock, Massachusetts.

As in all things Shaker, the case and dial are very plain, with no decoration or adornment. This clock may be made with a solid wood door panel like the original, or a glass panel may be used in order to reveal the pendulum action.

Material List

Part		Number	Size
A	Sides	2	4" x 30⅝" x ¾"
B	Top/base	2	6" x 14½" x ¾"
C	Back	1	11" x 30⅝" x ⅜"
D	Divider	1	6" x 12½" x ⅝"
E	Hanger	½	5" dia. circle x ⅝"
F	Top door	1	12½" x 12½" x ¾"
G	Lower door	1	12½" x 18" x ¾"
H	Wood panel	1	10½" x 16" x ⅜"

10" square dial, very plain
Glass panel, 10½" x 10½"
Movement of choice, 16" pendulum
Optional glass panel, 10½" x 16"

CONSTRUCTION

1. Lay out and cut Parts A, B, C, and D to shape and size. Cut a ⅜" x ⅜" rabbet on the rear inside edges of Parts A. Cut a pendulum slot in Part D. (See assembly drawing for detail.) Nail or screw Parts B into Parts A. Nail Part C into the rabbets in Parts A. Fit Part D as shown in the assembly drawing and nail Parts A and C into Part D. Nail the top, Part B, into Part E.

2. Make two doors using 1¼" wide stiles and rails. Use half-lap, spline, or dowel joinery. Cut a glass rabbet into the top door. Secure glass into this rabbet with wood strips or glazier's points. Cut a ⅜" deep panel rabbet into the bottom door. Secure a wood panel in this rabbet by means of thin wood strips nailed inside the doorframe. *Note: Glass may be used in place of the wood panel for the bottom door. If this is the case, follow the directions for a glass rabbet and glass attachment.* Secure the doors to Parts A using 1¼" x 1¼" brass butt hinges. Attach catches and small wood pulls.

Isaac Young Wall Clock. Hancock Shaker Village, Inc., Hancock, Massachusetts.

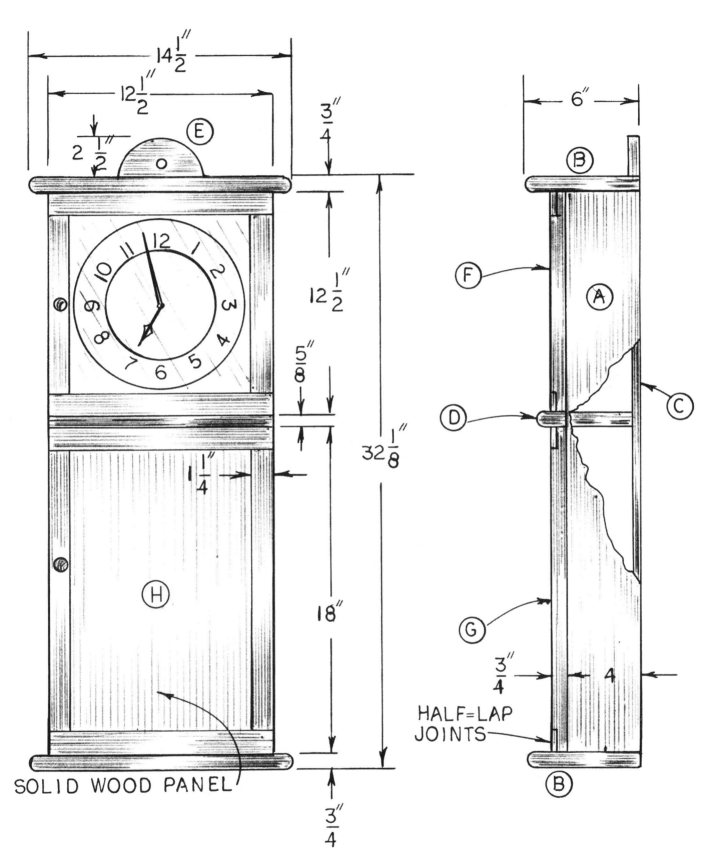

14$\frac{1}{2}$"

12$\frac{1}{2}$"

E

2$\frac{1}{2}$"

3$\frac{1}{4}$"

12$\frac{1}{2}$"

$\frac{5}{8}$"

32$\frac{1}{8}$"

1$\frac{1}{4}$"

H

18"

SOLID WOOD PANEL

$\frac{3}{4}$"

6"

B

F

A

D

C

G

$\frac{3}{4}$"

4

HALF=LAP
JOINTS

B

Shaker wall clock front and side views.

147

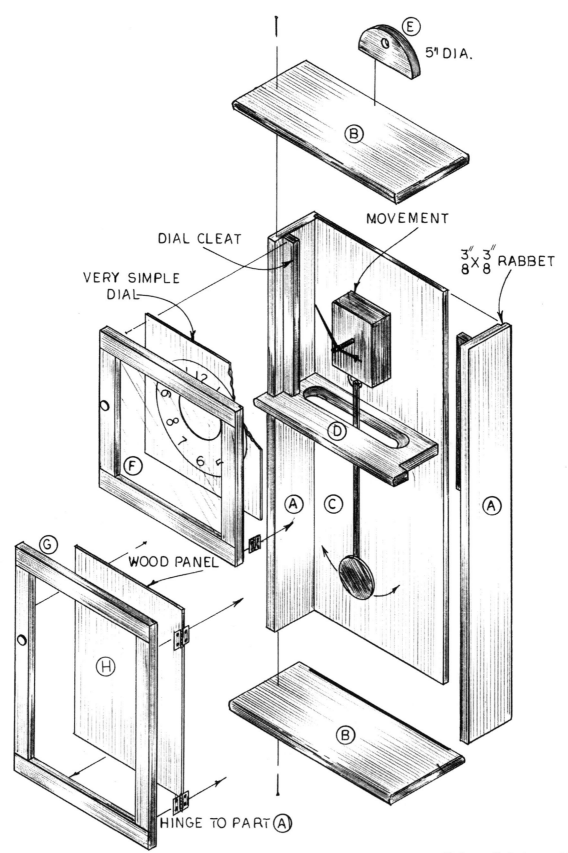

E 5" DIA.

B

DIAL CLEAT

MOVEMENT

VERY SIMPLE
DIAL

$\frac{3''}{8} \times \frac{3''}{8}$ RABBET

F

12
6
9
8
7
6

A C

D

A

G

WOOD PANEL

H

HINGE TO PART A

B

Shaker wall clock assembly plan.

148

3. Make a dial cleat or frame from 1½" wide stock. Nail or screw this frame between Parts A, ½" back from the front edges. Secure a pendulum movement of choice in the central top door area. Glue or fixture blocks may be required for heavy movements. Secure the chosen dial to the cleat frame with screws or brads. *Note: A battery replacement access hole can be cut into the back of the case if desired; otherwise, battery replacement can be achieved by removing the dial.*

4. Set and fill all nailheads. Cover all exposed screwheads with plugs. Sand entire reproduction smooth. Stain or paint to a color of choice. Cover with a flat or satin finish. (See Appendix under *Finishing* for suggestions.)

Shaker-style Wall Clock
(Circa mid-1800s)

The Shakers did not believe in decorations or fancy moldings on their furnishings. Most often their pieces were kept very simple, unadorned, and functional. The beauty of the following clock is based upon Shaker simplicity in design.

Material List

Part	Number	Size
A Sides	2	3¼" x 30½" x ¾"
B Ends	2	5¼" x 12" x ¾"
C Back	1	9¼" x 30½" x ⅜"
D Front	1	10" x 30½" x ¾"
E Hanger	1	3" x 4½" x ¾"
F Cove molding	1	1" x 12" x ¾"
	2	1" x 4¾" x ¾"

7" or 8" dia. dial/bezel combination (very simple dial)
Movement of choice with 16" or 18" pendulum
Glass panel, 1¼" x 7"

CONSTRUCTION

1. Lay out and cut Parts A and B to shape and size. Round over the front edge and both ends of Parts B. Cut a ⅜" x ⅜" rabbet on the rear inside edges of Part A. Nail or screw Parts B into Parts A. Form Part E and nail or screw the top Part B into Part E. Nail Part C into the rabbets on Parts A. Note movement access hole in Part C. (See assembly drawing for detail.)

2. Make the front panel, Part D, to shape and size. Lay out the bezel frame to size and cut an access seat or hole for movement. Cut a rounded slot for the pendulum view. The slot location will be determined by the length of the pendulum shaft used. Secure a glass panel behind this slot using thin wood stops. Secure Part D to Parts A with nails or screws. Cut the cove molding, Parts F, to size. Make 45° miter corners. Nail Parts F to Parts A, D, and the top, Part B.

3. Set and fill all nail heads. Cover all screw-heads with plugs. Sand entire reproduction smooth. Stain or paint to a color of choice. Cover with a flat or satin-type finish. (See Appendix under *Finishing* for suggestions.) Secure the movement to the bezel/dial by means of a threaded nut and the threaded hand shaft stem. Secure the bezel/dial/movement assembly to Part D. Install a wall hanger.

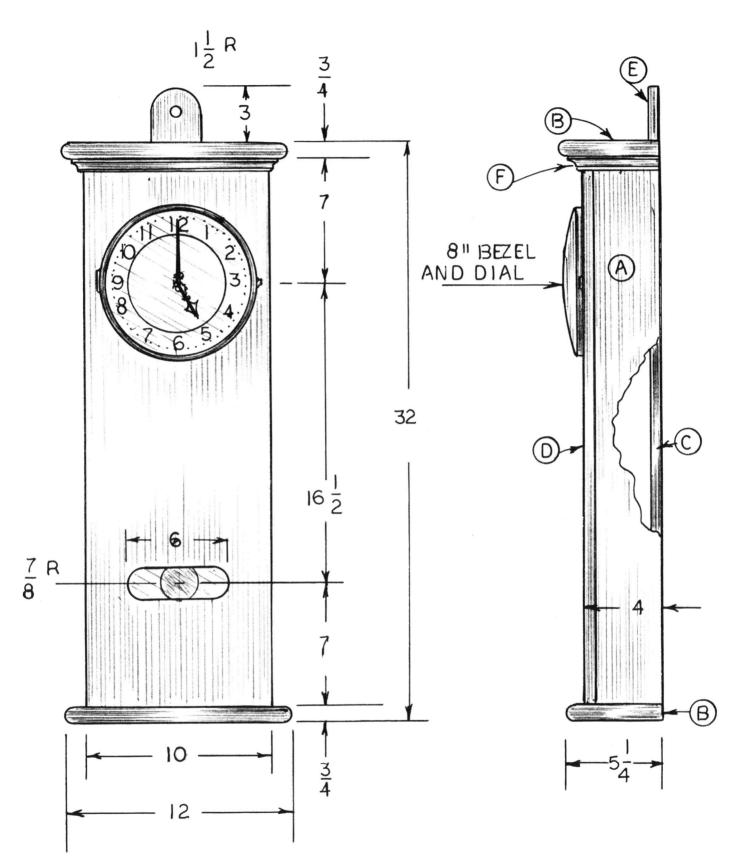

Shaker-style wall clock front and side views.

151

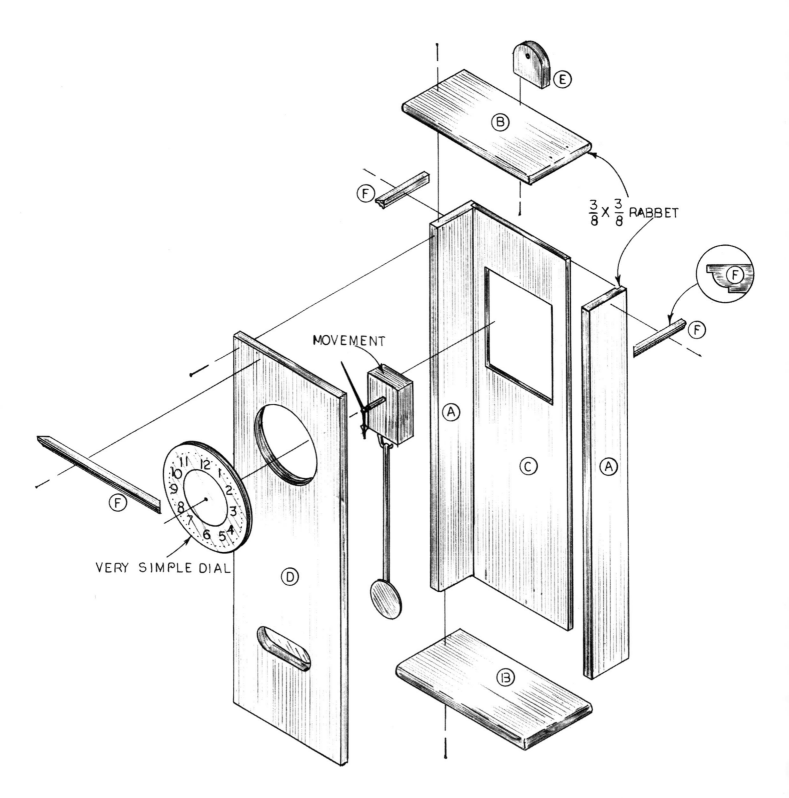

MOVEMENT

VERY SIMPLE DIAL

$\frac{3}{8} \times \frac{3}{8}$ RABBET

Ⓐ Ⓑ Ⓒ Ⓓ Ⓔ Ⓕ

10 11 12 1 2 3 4 5 6 7 8 9

Shaker-style wall clock assembly plan.

152

SECTION FOUR

Tall Case Clocks

New England-style Grandmother Clock (Circa mid-1700s)

The clocks once known only as "Tall Case" or "Hall" clocks are now commonly referred to as grandfather, grandmother, or granddaughter clocks. The major difference among the three categories is the overall height of the cases. The three may have moving moon dials, chiming tones, and decorative pendulums. The shorter versions seem to fit better in contemporary rooms.

The following reproduction was developed from several 18th-century museum pieces. The design employs a square dial rather than a moon dial arch, yet it retains the graceful swan-neck scroll, majestic use of moldings, a carved eagle plaque, and the grace of a well-turned finial, all favorite designs of Colonial Americans.

Material List

Part		Number	Size
A	Base sides	2	8¼" x 16½" x ¾"
A1	Base bottom	1	8¼" x 14¼" x ¾"
B	Front panel (base)	1	15" x 15¾" x ¾"
C	Front skirt	1	3½" x 16½" x ¾"
D	Side skirts	2	3½" x 9¾" x ¾"
E	Shelf ledger	1	3½" x 18½" x ¾"
		2	3½" x 11½" x ¾"
F	Waist sides	2	6¾" x 35" x ¾"
G	Hood sides	2	8¼" x 15" x ¾"
H	Top	1	12" x 18½" x ¾"
I	Top ledger	1	2¾" x 19" x ¾"
		2	2¾" x 11½" x ¾"
J	Pediment	1	6¼" x 13½" x ¾"
K	Pediment sides	2	2¾" x 9" x ¾"
	Rosettes	2	2" dia. x ½"
	Swan-neck	2	¾" x 6" x ¾"
	Side molds	2	¾" x 9" x ¾"
L	Finial	1	1¾" dia. x 3¾"
M	Cove molding	15 feet	¾" x ¾"
N	Back panel	1	14¼" x 65½" x ⅜"
O	Dial door	1	13½" x 13½" x ¾"
P	Waist door	1	12" x 25½" x ¾"
Q	Waist header	1	4" x 12" x ¾"

11" x 11" square dial
Movement of choice with 25" pendulum
Clear glass panel, 11½" x 11½" (dial door)
Clear glass panel, 8½" x 22" (waist door)
Carved eagle (see patterns)
Small door pulls (2), brass
Door catches of choice (2)
Optional: decorative weight shells, if quartz movement is used; decorative pendulum

Cherry grandmother clock. Author's collection.

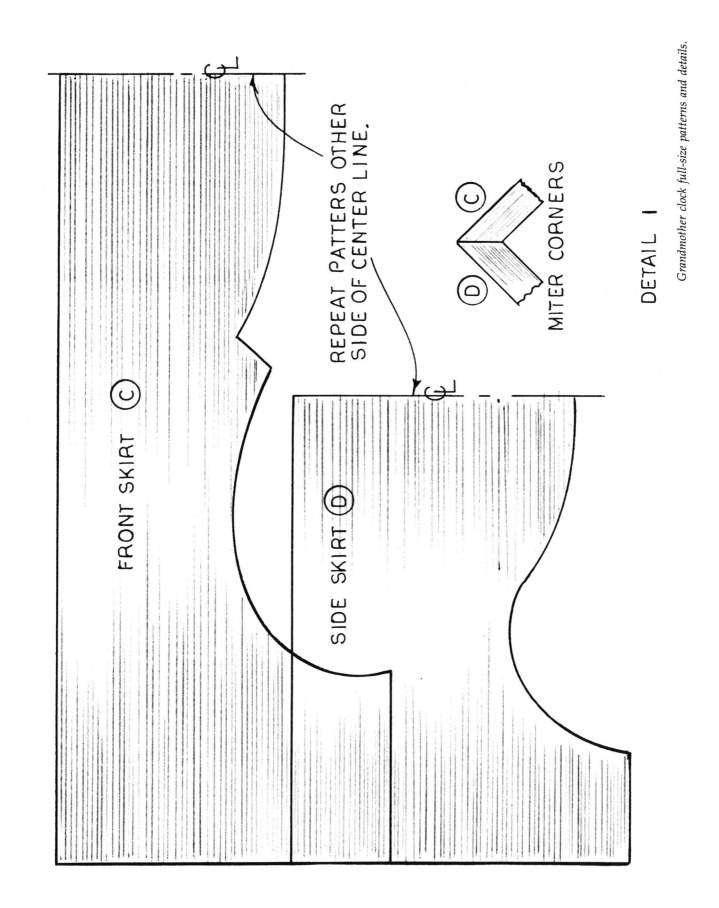

FRONT SKIRT Ⓒ

SIDE SKIRT Ⓓ

REPEAT PATTERS OTHER
SIDE OF CENTER LINE.

CL

CL

MITER CORNERS

Ⓒ

Ⓓ

DETAIL 1

Grandmother clock full-size patterns and details.

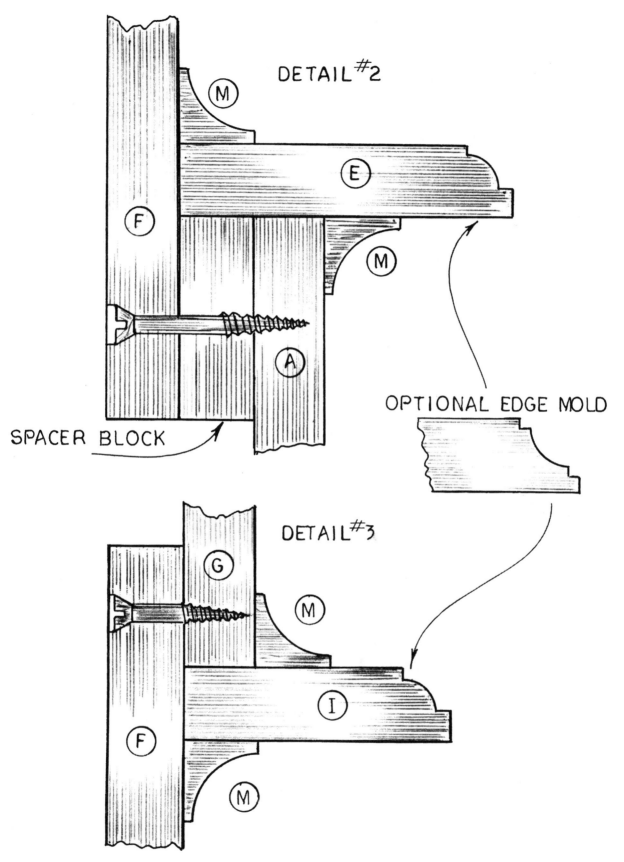

DETAIL #2

M

E

F

M

A

SPACER BLOCK

OPTIONAL EDGE MOLD

DETAIL #3

G

M

F

I

M

Grandmother clock full-size patterns and details.

157

CONSTRUCTION

1. Study the plans and patterns carefully before starting work. This grandmother clock is made in three stages: the base; the waist, or midsection; and the hood, or top section. The common molding used on all connecting sections may be any molding of choice or preference. While cove or scotia molding is shown, any design of the same size can be substituted. The moldings can be shop-made with a shaper or router, purchased as stock items from lumberyards, or purchased from clock suppliers.

2. Lay out and cut Parts A, A1, B, C, and D to shape and size. (See full-size patterns for Parts C and D.) Cut a ⅜" rabbet on the rear inside edges of Parts A and A-1. Glue and screw Parts A into Part A-1. Make a raised panel section consisting of 2" wide stiles and 3" wide rails. The various moldings will cover part of the rails and the remaining exposed amount (2") will be equal to the exposed stile width. Half-lap joints are suggested for making this raised panel frame. Cut a ⅜" x ⅜" rabbet into the inside edges of this frame and secure a raised panel into the rabbets. Screw the finished frame (with raised panel) into Parts A.

3. Using 45° miter joints, cut and screw Parts C and D to Parts A and the bottom inch of Part B. Glue a ¾" wide by 2¼" x 6½" spacer block to the top of Parts A. (See detail #2 in the full-size patterns for suggestions.)

4. Lay out and cut Parts E and F to suggested shape and size. Cut a ⅜" x ⅜" rabbet into the rear inside edges of Parts F. Glue and screw Parts F to the spacer blocks and bottom assembly with all the back edges in a plumb line to each other. With a router, cut a decorative outer edge on Parts E. Parts E are joined using 45° miter joints. Screw Parts E into Parts A and F. Screw a ¾" x ¾" spacer between Parts F and on top of the front Part E. Using 45° miter joints, cut the molding, Parts M, and nail these moldings in place around the section joint.

5. Lay out and cut Parts G, H, and I to sug-gested shape and size. With a router, cut a decorative or molded edge on Parts H and I. Parts I are joined using 45° miters. Cut a ⅜" x ⅜" rabbet on the rear inside edges of Parts G and H. Part H rabbet is blind. Screw Parts G into Parts F. (See detail #3 in full-size patterns for suggestions.) Screw Part H down into Parts G. Screw Parts I to Parts F and G. Cut the required moldings, Parts M, and secure them in place around the joint with nails. A ¾" x ¾" backer strip may be installed behind the front top and bottom Parts M, just under Part H and just over the front Part I. Lay out and make the pediment, Parts J, K, and L. (See full-size patterns in detail #6.) Using dowel pins, glue the finished Parts J and K to the top of Part H.

6. Lay out and cut the back, Part N, to shape and size. Part N fits into the rabbets cut in Parts A, A1, F, G, and H. Nail or screw Part N in place. Cut and fit Part Q to the top waist piece and screw Part Q to Parts F. Purchase or carve an eagle or similar decorative panel, or use any other suitable decorative insert and attach it to the center of Part Q. (See full-size pattern for the eagle design.)

7. Make a top door, Part O. Use half-lap joints on 1½" wide rails and stiles. Cut a glass rabbet on the rear inside edges of the door-frame. Install this door to Part G with 1" x 1" brass butt hinges.

8. Make a waist section door, Part P. Use 2" wide rails and stiles, and half-lap joints for this construction. Cut a glass rabbet in the rear inside edges of the finished door. Secure the door to Part F using three 1¼" x 2" brass butt hinges. Install glass in both door rabbets using thin wood stops or glazier's points.

9. Make a dial backer board and install it ½" back from the front edges of Parts G. Install a movement of choice and selected clock dial. The movement, depending upon selection, may require a wood seat board cut with a slot to allow for the weight-drive chains. This seat board, if needed, should be firmly secured to Part G. The size, location, and design of this seat board will vary depending upon the make

OPTIONAL DESIGN

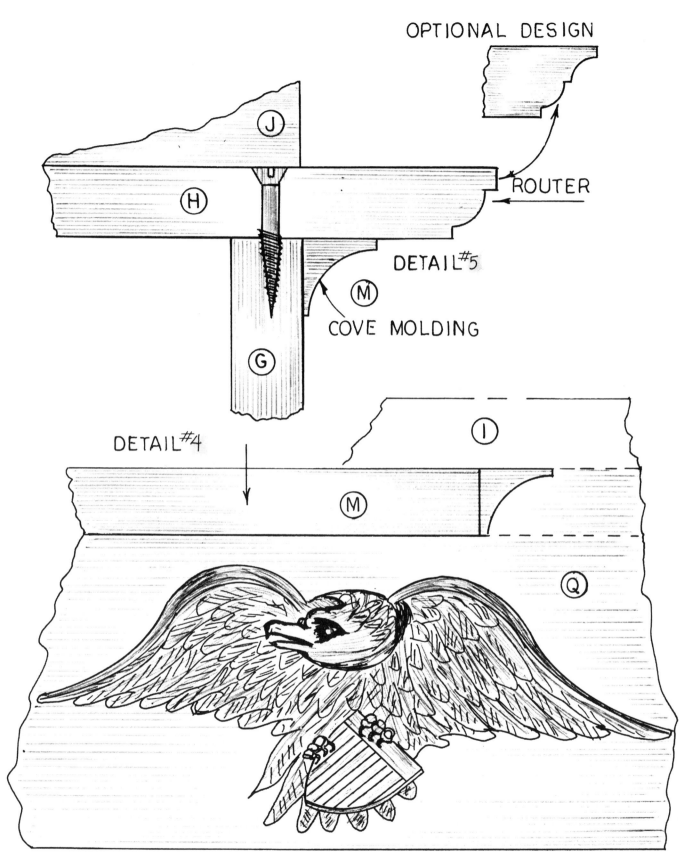

ROUTER

DETAIL#5

J

H

G

M

COVE MOLDING

DETAIL#4

I

M

Q

Grandmother clock full-size patterns and details.

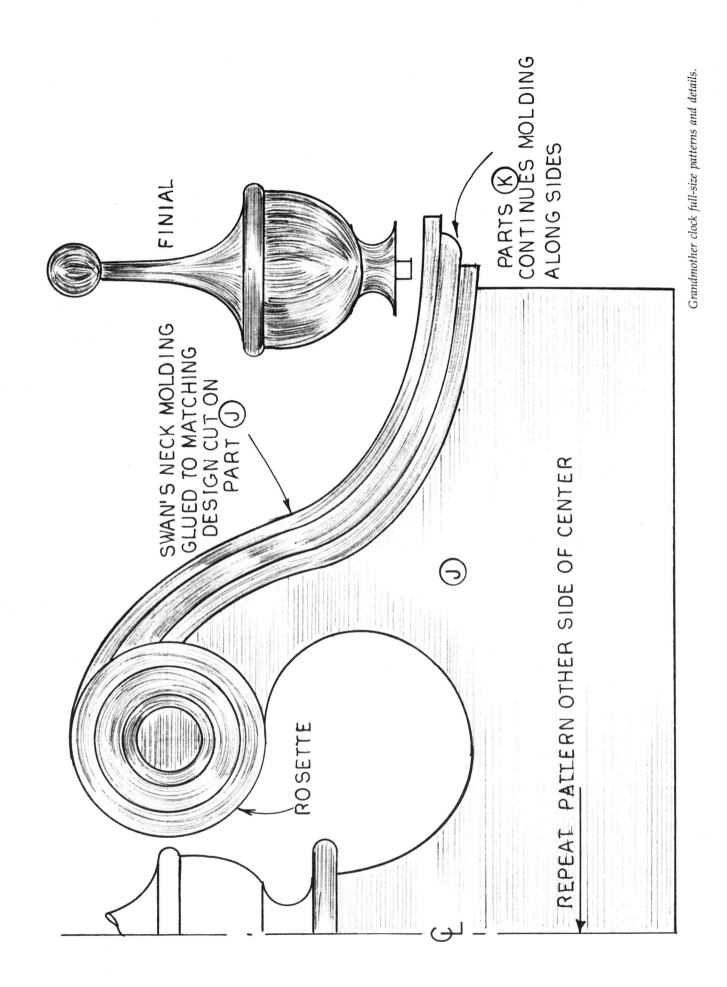

FINIAL

SWAN'S NECK MOLDING
GLUED TO MATCHING
DESIGN CUT ON
PART J

ROSETTE

J

PARTS K
CONTINUES MOLDING
ALONG SIDES

REPEAT PATTERN OTHER SIDE OF CENTER

Grandmother clock full-size patterns and details.

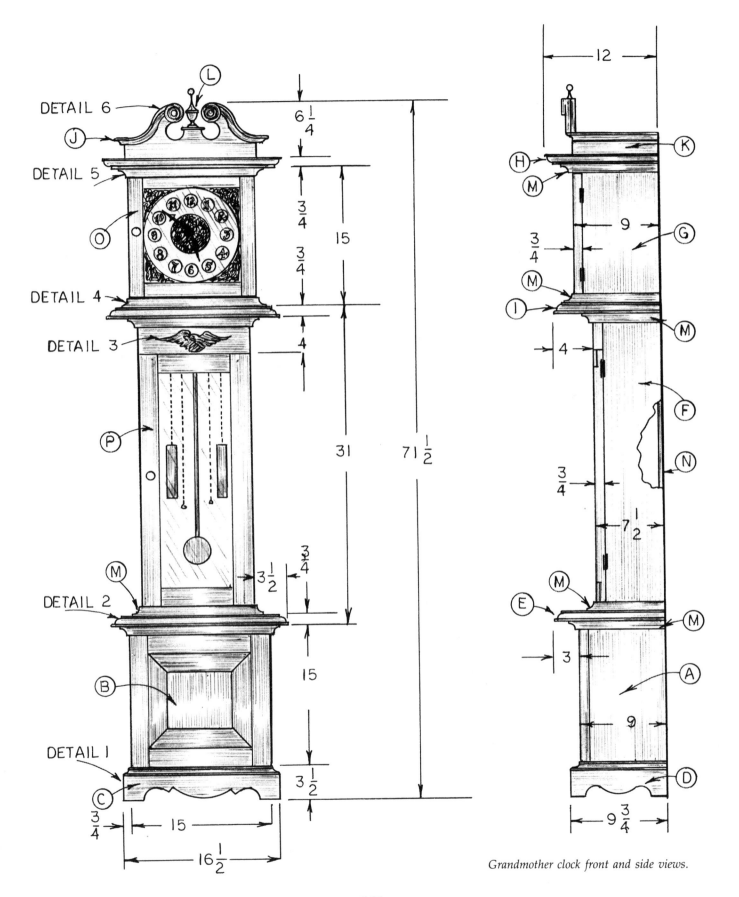

DETAIL 6

DETAIL 5

DETAIL 4

DETAIL 3

DETAIL 2

DETAIL 1

$6\frac{1}{4}$

$\frac{3}{4}$

$\frac{3}{4}$

15

4

31

$71\frac{1}{2}$

$\frac{3}{4}$

$3\frac{1}{2}$

15

$3\frac{1}{2}$

$\frac{3}{4}$

15

$16\frac{1}{2}$

12

9

$\frac{3}{4}$

4

$\frac{3}{4}$

$7\frac{1}{2}$

3

9

$9\frac{3}{4}$

Grandmother clock front and side views.

161

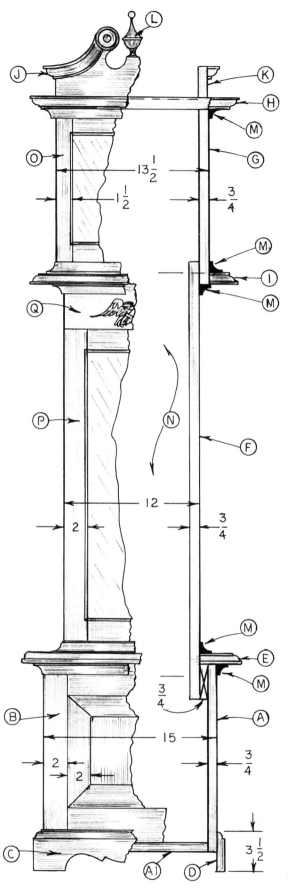

Grandmother clock sectional view.

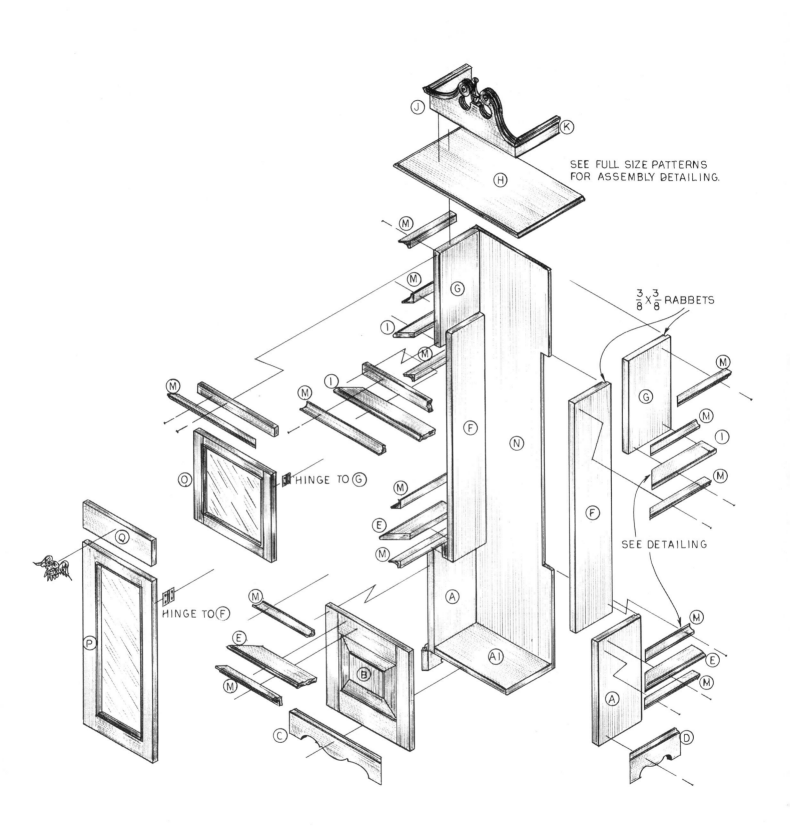

SEE FULL SIZE PATTERNS FOR ASSEMBLY DETAILING.

$\frac{3}{8}$ X $\frac{3}{8}$ RABBETS

SEE DETAILING

HINGE TO G

HINGE TO F

Grandmother clock assembly plan.

and nature of the movement used. (See manufacturer's instructions for such information.)

10. Finish. Remove movement, dial, and glass. Set and fill any nailheads. Cover all exposed screwheads with plugs made from the same wood species used to make the clock case. Sand the entire reproduction smooth. Stain to a color of choice. Cover with several coats of lacquer or other favorite finish. (See instruction for finishing in Appendix for suggestions.) Reinstall the dial, glass, and movement. Set the finished clock in its selected place. Using a level, plumb the clock so that it sits level and firm in its assigned spot. Shims may be required under the skirt board if the floor is uneven. It is not unheard of to secure the clock in place with a screw through the backer piece into a house wall stud, to prevent accidental upsetting.

Shaker Tall Case Clock (Circa early 1800s)

The following Shaker reproduction was designed from a very rare Shaker tall case clock which is now in The Shaker Museum in Old Chatham, New York. True to the Shaker tradition, the case is very simple, allowing only the limited use of plain cove moldings. The dial displays hour and minute indicators only, without any additional embellishment. While the original Erastus Rude tall case had a high dial arch where normally a moon dial would appear, this offering was designed with a square dial and optional top crown.

This same basic design and size was used for the following Pennsylvania Dutch hall clock.

Material List

	Part	Number	Size
A	Sides	2	8″ x 43″ x ¾″
B	Base sides	2	10″ x 16″ x ¾″
B1	Baseboard	1	10″ x 14½″ x ¾″
C	Front	1	16″ x 16″ x ¾″
D	Top sides	2	8¾″ x 14″ x ¾″
E	Back	1	15¼″ x 68½″ x ⅜″
F	Ledger	1	3″ x 19″ x ¾″
F1	Top	1	11″ x 18″ x ¾″
G	Cove molding	2	1¾″ x 1¾″ x 16″
		4	1¾″ x 1¾″ x 10″
H	Crown (optional)	1	4″ x 15″ x ¾″
I	Crown sides	2	2″ x 8″ x ¾″
J	Waist frame	2	2″ x 38½″ x ¾″
		2	4″ x 8″ x ¾″
K	Waist door	1	8″ x 31¼″ x ¾″
L	Dial door	1	14″ x 14″ x ¾″

Square dial, 11″ x 11″, very plain and simple
Movement of choice (pendulum optional)
Glass panel, 13″ x 13″, single-strength

CONSTRUCTION

1. Review full-size patterns and detailing before starting work. Note the placement of various parts, and note the cove molding. Such molding may be shop-made, purchased from local lumberyards, or purchased from clock supply outlets.

2. Lay out and cut Parts A, B, C, and D to shape and size. Cut a ⅜″ x ⅜″ rabbet into the rear inside edges of Parts A, B, and D. Keeping all the rear edges in a straight line, glue and screw Parts A into Parts D. (See detail #2 for full-size patterns.) Using a ¾″ thick spacer block, glue and screw Parts A into Parts B. (See detail #1 for placement and full-size patterns.) Make a pair of matching assemblies using Parts A, B, and D.

3. Lay out and cut Part E, the back, to size and shape. Nail Part E into the rabbets cut into the two assemblies, Parts A, B, and D. Part E will tie the two assemblies together in a square, plumb alignment. Screw Parts B into Part B1. Screw Part C into Parts B.

4. Lay out and cut Parts F and F1 to shape and size. Screw Part F1 down into Parts D. Nail Part F into the bottoms of Parts D. (See detail #2.) Using 45° miter corners, cut the cove molding and install Parts G as shown in details #1 and #2.

5. The crown and crown sides, Parts H and I, are optional and do not appear on the original Shaker clock. If used, lay out and cut Parts

Erastus Rude Tall Case Clock. Shaker Museum, Old Chatham, New York.

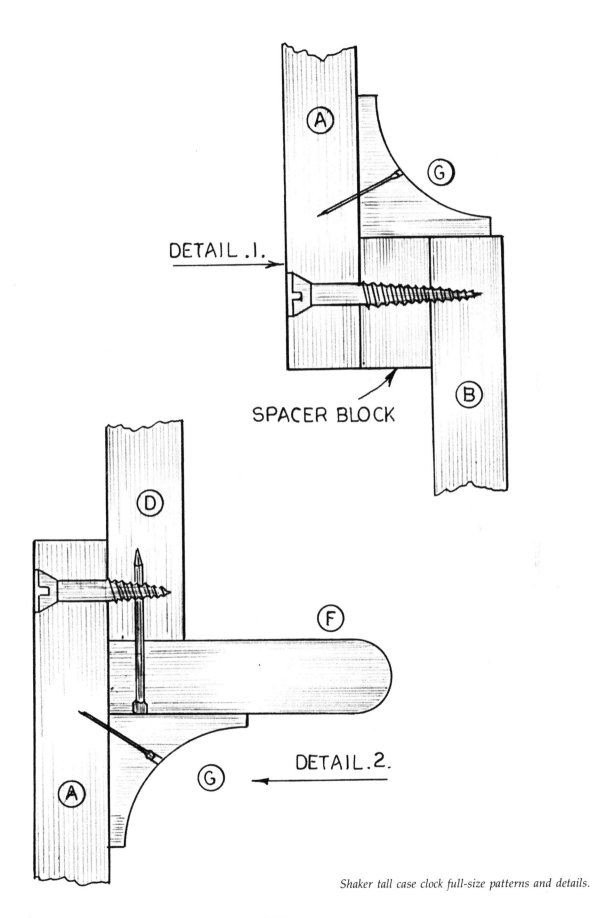

DETAIL .I.

SPACER BLOCK

DETAIL. 2.

Shaker tall case clock full-size patterns and details.

167

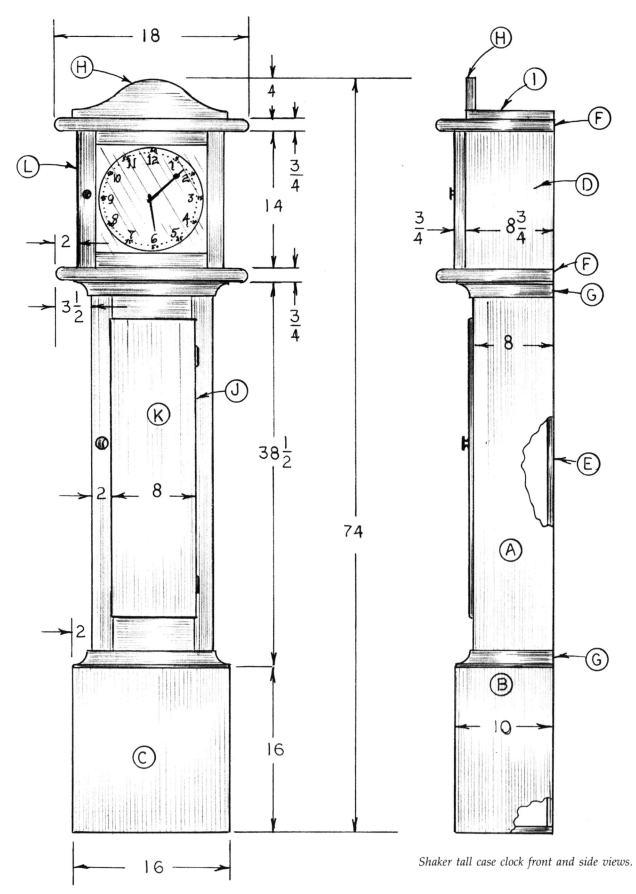

Shaker tall case clock front and side views.

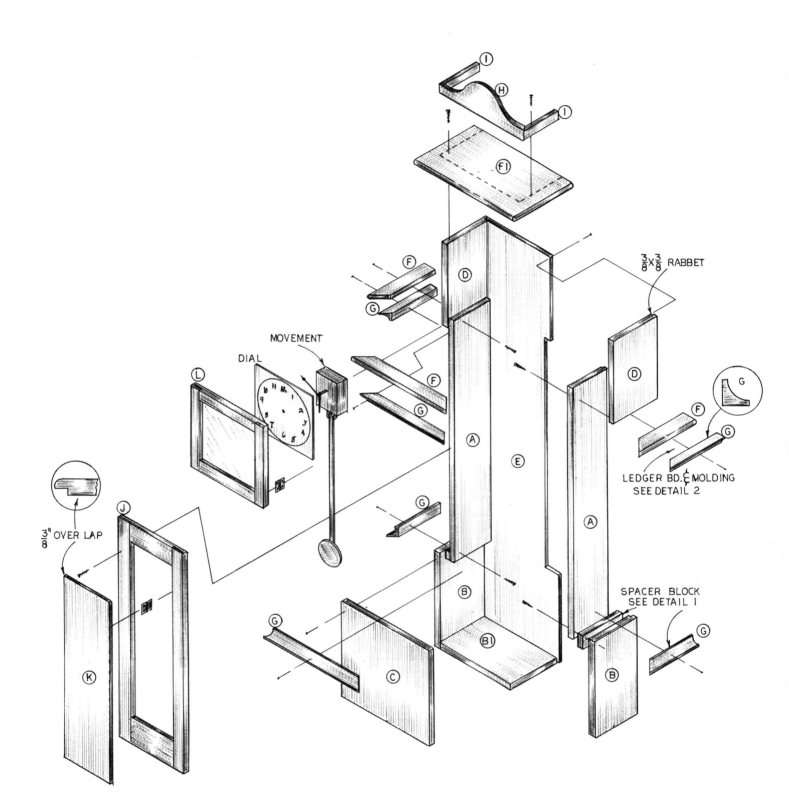

Shaker tall case clock assembly plan.

$\frac{3}{8} \times \frac{3}{8}$ RABBET

LEDGER BD. & MOLDING
SEE DETAIL 2

MOVEMENT

DIAL

$\frac{3}{8}$" OVER LAP

SPACER BLOCK
SEE DETAIL 1

H and I to shape and size. Using 45° miters, make the required joints and screw Parts H and I into Part F1.

6. Lay out and cut Parts J to desired size. Make a frame from these parts and nail or screw the finished frame to Parts A. Cut a solid wood door, Part K, and make ⅜" x ⅜" overlap rabbets on all four sides. Install the finished door to the waist frame, Parts J, with ⅜" offset or inset hinges. Install a door catch and pull.

7. Make a dial door using 1½" rails and stiles. Use half-lap joinery. Cut a glass rabbet on the rear inside edges. Install a glass panel using glazier's points or thin wood strips. Install the door to Parts D with 1" x 1" brass butt hinges. Install a catch and pull.

8. Install a dial frame or series of cleats made of 2" wide stock. Make a frame and secure it to Parts D with screws. Mount the movement of your choice within the frame and centered to the glass area of the dial door. Install a dial over the movement, attached to the dial frame.

9. Remove the dial, movement, and glass. Set and fill any nailheads. Cover any exposed screwheads with plugs. Sand entire reproduction smooth. Stain or paint to a color of choice. *Note: Some Shaker furnishings were painted a dull yellow or red, and this clock may be so treated if preferred.* (See Appendix under *Finishing* for suggestions.) After finishing, reinstall the movement, dial, and door glass. (While the original Shaker clock had a solid wood door for the waist, Part K, a glass panel door may be used if preferred.)

Pennsylvania Dutch
Tall Case Clock
(Circa late 1700s)

The following tall case clock was developed from the basic Shaker tall case clock measurements. This Pennsylvania Dutch–style clock offers a broken pediment, skirt boards, turned columns, and a bottom ledger board. Other than these additions, the dimensions and part numbers are the same as those given for the Shaker tall case clock.

While the Shakers were very austere in their furnishings, the Pennsylvania Dutch went to the extreme in bright decorating. They often covered their furnishings with flowers, birds, geometric constructions, or combinations of all three. Bright, fancy colors embellished most common household items. One authority said, "They make music on the eye and laughter in the heart." This reproduction may be stained or painted, and the typical Pennsylvania designs may be applied with bright paints or decals if preferred.

Material List

Part		Number	Size
A	Sides	2	8″ x 43″ x ¾″
B	Base sides	2	10″ x 16″ x ¾″
B1	Base	1	10″ x 14½″ x ¾″
B2	Skirt boards	1	3″ x 18″ x ¾″
		2	3″ x 11″ x ¾″
C	Front board	1	16″ x 16″ x ¾″
D	Top sides	2	8¾″ x 14″ x ¾″
E	Back	1	15¼″ x 68½″ x ⅜″
F	Ledgers	2	3″ x 19″ x ¾″
		4	3″ x 13″ x ¾″
F1	Top	1	11″ x 18″ x ¾″
F2	Columns	4	1″ dia. x 14½″
G	Cove moldings	2	1¾″ x 1¾″ x 16″
		4	1¾″ x 1¾″ x 10″
H	Pediment	1	6″ x 16″ x ¾″
		2	2½″ x 8″ x ¾″
I	Finial	1	2″ dia. x 4″
J	Waist frame	2	2″ x 38½″ x ¾″
		2	4″ x 8″ x ¾″
K	Waist door	1	8″ x 31¼″ x ¾″
L	Dial door	1	14″ x 14″ x ¾″

Square dial, 11″ x 11″, floral or scroll design
Movement of choice with pendulum
Glass panel, 13″ x 13″
Brass finial, 2″ dia. x 3½″ (optional)

CONSTRUCTION

1. Lay out and cut Parts A, B, B1, B2, C, and D to suggested shape and size. (See full-size patterns for the skirt board designs.) Cut a ⅜″ x ⅜″ rabbet on the rear inside edge of Parts A, B, and D. Keeping all the back edges in a straight line, glue and screw Parts A into Parts D. (See detail in full-size patterns.) Using a ¾″ thick spacer block, glue and screw Parts A

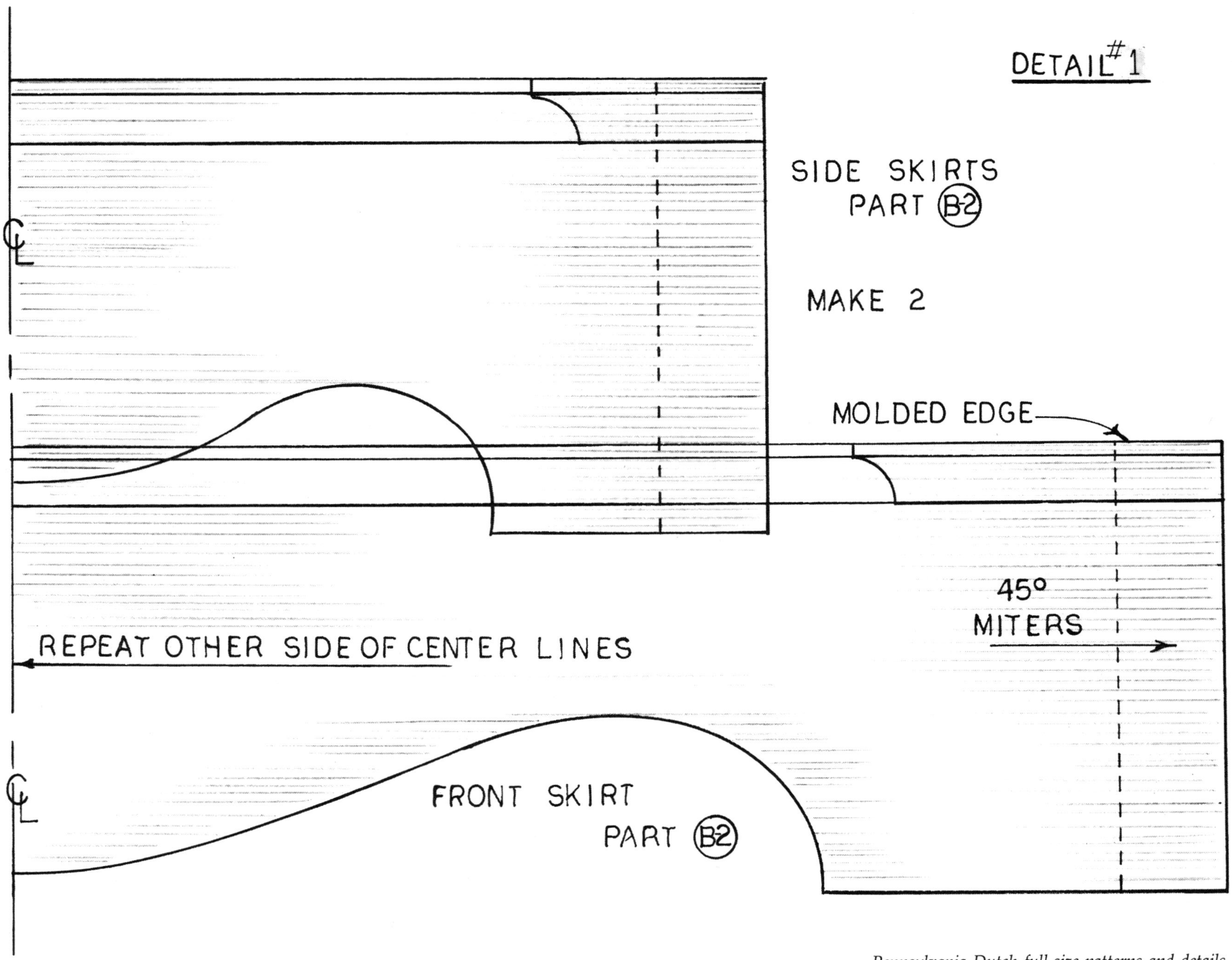

DETAIL #1

SIDE SKIRTS
PART B2

MAKE 2

MOLDED EDGE

45°
MITERS

FRONT SKIRT
PART B2

REPEAT OTHER SIDE OF CENTER LINES

CL

CL

Pennsylvania Dutch full-size patterns and details.

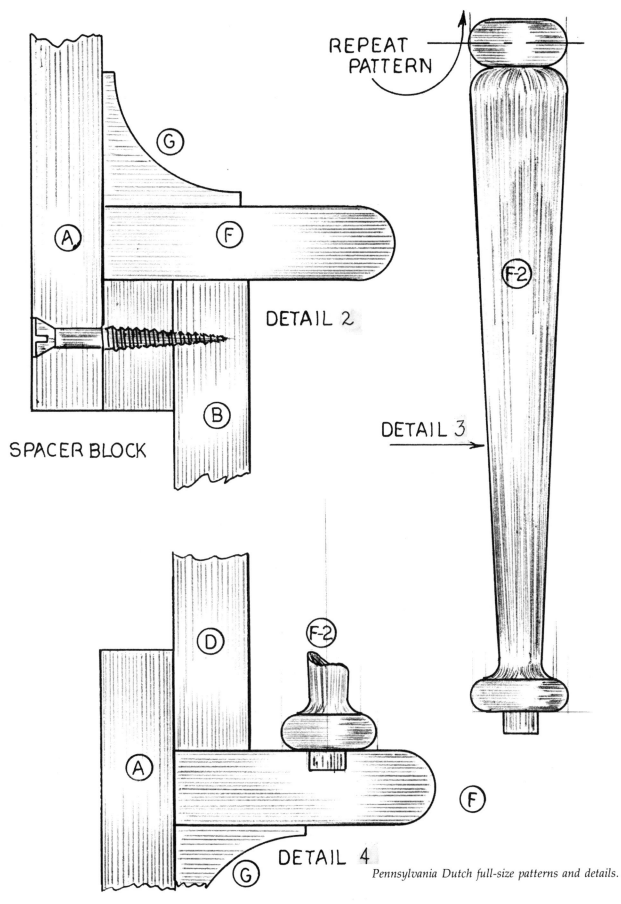

REPEAT PATTERN

G

A

F

DETAIL 2

SPACER BLOCK

B

F-2

DETAIL 3

D

F-2

A

F

DETAIL 4

G

Pennsylvania Dutch full-size patterns and details.

173

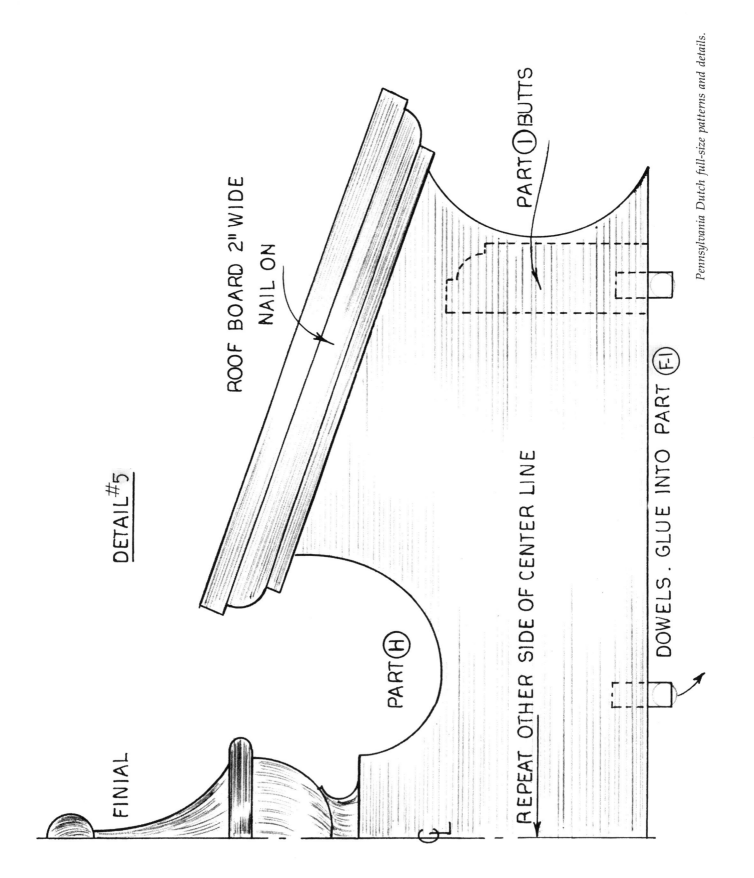

DETAIL #5

ROOF BOARD 2" WIDE
NAIL ON

PART ① BUTTS

FINIAL

PART ⓗ

REPEAT OTHER SIDE OF CENTER LINE

C̶L̶

DOWELS. GLUE INTO PART Ⓕ-1

Pennsylvania Dutch full-size patterns and details.

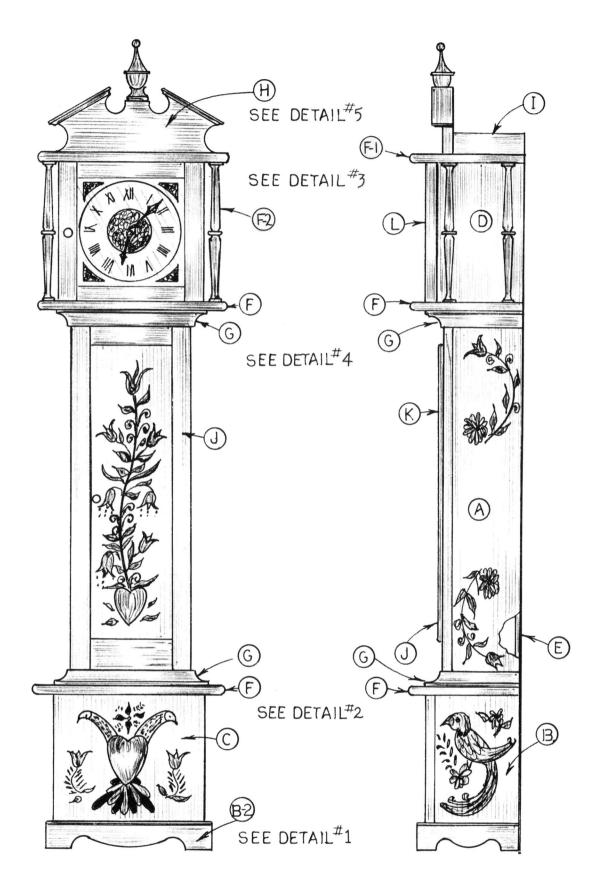

SEE DETAIL#5

SEE DETAIL#3

SEE DETAIL#4

SEE DETAIL#2

SEE DETAIL#1

NOTE – ALL SIZES THE SAME AS THOSE GIVEN FOR SHAKER CLOCK.

Pennsylvania Dutch front and side views.

into Parts B. (See detail in full-size patterns.) Make a pair of matching assemblies of Parts A, B, and D.

2. Lay out and cut Part E to size. Nail Part E into the rabbets cut into Parts A, B, and D. Part E will tie the two side assemblies together in square alignment. Screw the bottom of Parts B into Part B1. Screw Part C into Parts B and B1.

3. Lay out and cut Parts B2 to shape and size. (See full-size patterns.) Screw the finished skirts into Parts C and B. Use 45° mitered corners for the skirt boards.

4. Lay out and cut Parts F and F1 to shape and size. Screw Parts F down into Parts D. Screw Part F1 into Parts D and Parts B. (See detailing in full-size assembly drawings for the ledger boards.) Note the molded edge applied to the front and ends of Parts F and F1. Part F1 is secured using 45° mitered corners. Cut and install the cove molding around Part F1. (See location in full-size patterns.)

5. Lathe-turn or purchase four turned tapered columns, Parts F2. These columns have tenons on each end, which are inserted into mortise holes drilled into the bottom of Parts F and the top of Part F1. (See location in detail drawings.)

6. Lay out and cut Parts H to shape and size. (See instructions elsewhere in this book for making a swan-neck pediment. See detail plans for full-size patterns.) Using 45° mitered corners, glue and screw Parts H into the top of Part F1. Nail and glue the roof boards to the pediment peaks. Install a finial of choice.

7. Lay out and cut Parts J to desired size. Make a frame of these parts using half-lap joinery. Nail or screw the finished frame to Parts A, in between Parts F. Cut a solid wood door, Part K, and make ⅜" x ⅜" overlap rabbets on all four sides. Attach the finished door to the frame, Parts J, with ⅜" offset or inset hinges. Install a catch and pull.

8. Make a dial door using 1½" wide rails and stiles. Use butt, dowel, spline, or half-lap joints. Cut a glass rabbet on the inside rear edges. A molded exterior edge may be employed if desired. Install a glass panel in the glass rabbet using glazier's points or thin wood strips. Install the door to Parts D with 1" x 1" brass butt hinges. Install a catch and pull.

9. Install a dial frame made of 1½" wide stock. Screw this frame inside of Parts D, ½" back from the front edges. Mount the movement of choice in the center of this frame, and mount the dial over the movement.

10. Remove the dial, movement, and glass. Set and fill all nailheads. Cover all screwheads with plugs. Sand entire reproduction smooth. Stain or paint to a color of choice. *Note: Many Pennsylvania Dutch furnishings were painted. Medium green, blue, soft barn red, or yellow are possible colors.* (See Appendix under *Finishing* for possible antiquing suggestions. See notes on Pennsylvania styles in the Appendix.)

SECTION FIVE

Weather Stations

Weather instruments probably were developed in response to the needs of seafarers to predict meteorological conditions. Land travelers, too, have been aided through the development of accurate measurement and prediction of weather conditions.

A natural market for weather predicting instruments developed. One such instrument was the barometer, which shows barometric pressure and allows the user some degree of accuracy in his predictions. The following reproductions are examples of cases designed to house, protect, and display instruments for measuring humidity, barometric pressure, temperature, and sometimes time. Such a case, with instruments, is commonly called a weather station.

Sheraton-style Barometer (Circa mid-1700s)

Wall barometer. Old Wiggins Tavern, Hotel Northampton, Northampton, Massachusetts.

Material List

Plaque, 12″ x 35½″ x 1½″
Roof, 2″ x 3½″ x ¾″
Brass finial, 1½″ dia. x 2½″
Thermometer, 6″–8″ long
Hygrometer, 3″ dia. typical
Barometer, 8″–10″ dia. typical
Mirror, 3″–4″ dia. (optional)
Inlay, 1½″ dia. (optional)

CONSTRUCTION

1. Lay out and cut the main board to shape and size. Note grid design on 1″ squares. Sand all the edges smooth. A decorative molded edge may be applied with a router if desired. Make a broken pediment top with roof blocks. Cut a molded edge on the roof blocks. Nail these blocks to the pediment angles.

2. Mark out the location of the proposed instruments—barometer, hygrometer, or others—and cut any required relief holes into or through the main board. *Note: The barometer and hygrometer will require rear access to the atmosphere for proper operation.*

3. Stain to a color of choice and cover with several coats of lacquer or similar finish. (See Appendix for suggestions.) Install the thermometer, hygrometer, barometer, mirror, inlay, and finial. Install a wall hanger.

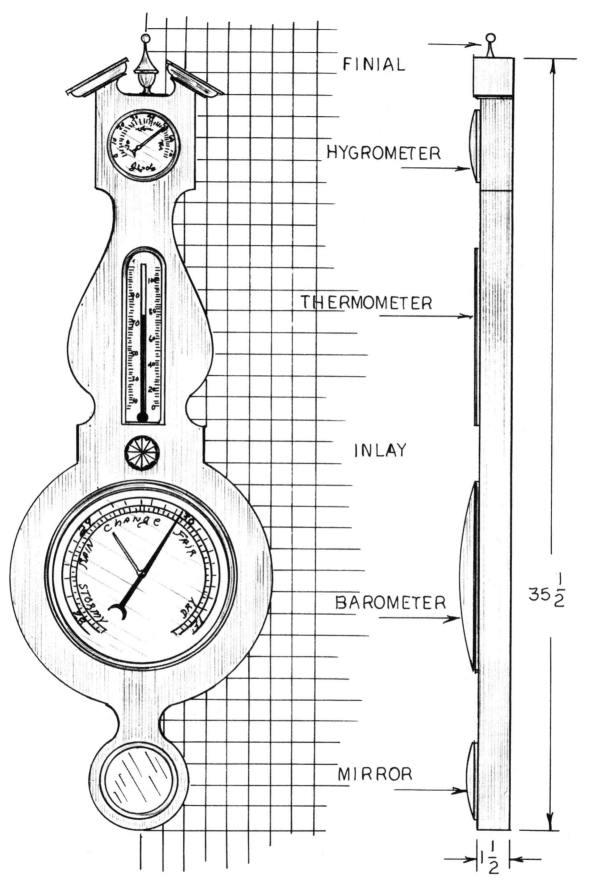

FINIAL

HYGROMETER

THERMOMETER

INLAY

BAROMETER

MIRROR

$35\frac{1}{2}$

$1\frac{1}{2}$

Sheraton-style barometer assembly plan.

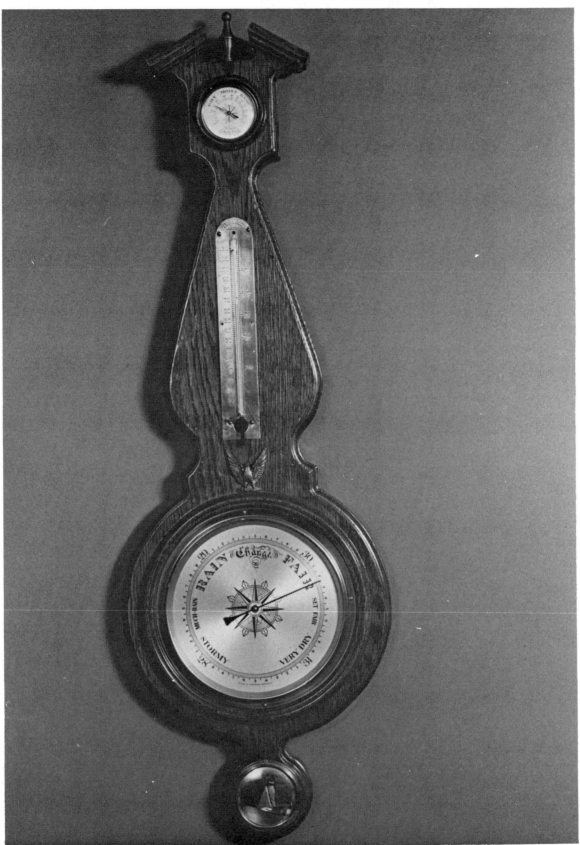

Oak Sheraton-style barometer.

Name Sign, Plaque-style Weather Station

This plaque was designed in the trade or name sign tradition in order to contain a round bezel-type weather instrument(s) and an 8″ diameter clock. The lower 4″ diameter bezels can be hygrometers, indoor/outdoor thermometers, or a small clock if used with an 8″ barometer. Any combination of instruments may be fitted to the station.

Material List

Note: The plaque center board is built out an additional ¾″ in order to allow room for the instrument backs.

Plaque, 14″ x 17″ x ¾″

Top, 5″ x 14″ x ¾″

Bottom, 3″ x 14″ x ¾″

Shelf, 3″ x 18″ x ¾″

8¼″ dia. bezel-style barometer or clock

4″ dia. hygrometer and barometer or clock

Thermometer may also be used if preferred.

CONSTRUCTION

1. Lay out and cut the suggested shape and size of the plaque center board. (See grid for design.) Lay out and cut the top and bottom pieces. Cut out the molded shelves. The molded edges are made with a router. Nail the main board into 1″ x 2″ side cleats in order to achieve suggested depth. Nail the top and bottom to the main board, and nail this plaque into the shelves as noted in drawing.

2. Drill out the required holes for the various instrument bezels.

3. Set and fill all nailheads. Sand entire weather plaque smooth. Stain or paint to a color of choice. (See Appendix for suggestion on finishing.) Attach the instruments with fasteners supplied by the manufacturer.

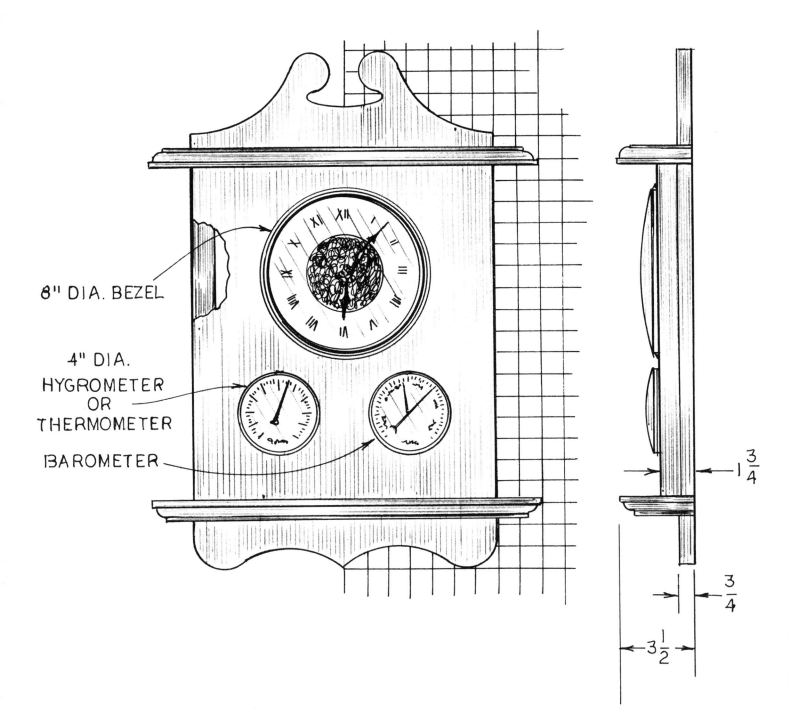

8" DIA. BEZEL

4" DIA.
HYGROMETER
OR
THERMOMETER

BAROMETER

$1\frac{3}{4}$

$\frac{3}{4}$

$3\frac{1}{2}$

Signboard-style weather station assembly plan.

182

Bezel-type barometer. Mason and Sullivan, West Yarmouth, Massachusetts.

Strip-style Weather Station

The following reproduction is designed to display 4″ diameter bezel-type instruments. The length of the backboard can be reduced or enlarged in order to accommodate a varying number of instruments, including a thermometer, barometer, hygrometer, exterior thermometer, mirror, or clock.

Material List

Part	Number	Size
Back board	1	8″ x 28¼″, typical
Edge moldings	2	2½″ x 9″ x ¾″
Pediment boards	2	1¾″ x 4″ x ⅝″

One each in 4″ dia.: thermometer, barometer, hygrometer, clock, or other of choice. Self-contained, bezel-type.

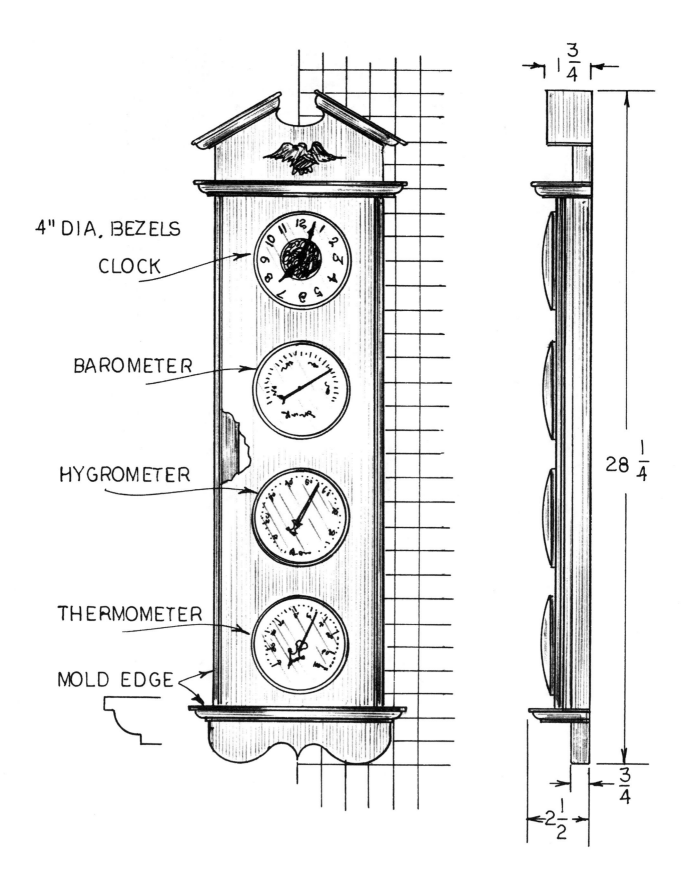

4" DIA. BEZELS

CLOCK

BAROMETER

HYGROMETER

THERMOMETER

MOLD EDGE

$1\frac{3}{4}$

$28\frac{1}{4}$

$\frac{3}{4}$

$2\frac{1}{2}$

Strip-style barometer assembly plan.

184

CONSTRUCTION

1. Lay out and cut the backboard to shape and size. (See grid design in assembly plan for sizes and design.) Nail backboard to the 1" x 2" suggested side cleats in order to produce depth for the instruments.

2. Lay out and cut the molded edge boards. Cut out the pediment roof boards. With a router, cut a selected molded edge on these parts. Nail the edge moldings to the backboards. Nail the roof boards to the pediment peaks.

3. Cut out the instrument seat holes for the bezels. Secure the instruments in place with fasteners provided by the suppliers.

4. Set and fill all nailheads. Sand entire weather station smooth. Stain or paint to a color of choice. Cover with several coats of lacquer or similar finish. (See Appendix under *Finishing* for suggestions.)

SECTION SIX

Appendix

SUPPLIERS OF CLOCK PARTS

The following list was developed as an aid for readers to acquire the needed movements, dials, hands, bezels, wood, and weather instruments needed for the reproductions offered in this book. Each company listed has displayed prompt, courteous service on my clock parts orders in the past. This is not, however, an unqualified endorsement of only these suppliers, because I am sure there are many other excellent clock parts supply companies who are just as reliable.

I recommend that you try local outlets or hobby and craft supply stores in your immediate area first. If local service is not available, then the listed national suppliers will sell and ship mail orders. Most of the listed suppliers offer catalogs or information sheets, and these should be obtained first, with mail-order lists made up after reviewing available choices.

Most clock parts are interchangeable to a degree; movements from one company, for example, will fit a dial from another vendor. I strongly recommend that the reader have the clock parts on hand—or at least a precise list of critical measurements, obtained from a company catalog—before starting work. Measurements may vary somewhat from company to company.

A suggestion is offered for each reproduction for the dial; bezel, if any; and movement. This is just a suggestion, however, and the reader is free to follow such recommendations, ignore them, or make substitutions.

Clock Parts Suppliers

Jules Borel Co.
1110 Grand Ave.
Kansas City, MO 64106
(816) 421–6110

Canadian Woodworker, Ltd.
1391 St. James St.
Winnipeg, Manitoba R3H 0Z1
Canada
(204) 786-3196

Cas-Ker Co.
2121 Spring Grove Ave.
Cincinnati, OH 45214
(513) 241-7073
1-800-487-0408

Albert Constantine & Son
2050 Eastchester Rd.
Bronx, NY 10461
(212) 792-1600

The American Clock Maker
2200 Dean St.
St. Charles, IL 60174
(715) 823-5101

Craftsman Wood Service Co.
1735 W. Cortland Ct.
Addison, IL 60101
1-800-543-9367

Emperor Clock Co.
Emperor Industrial Park
Fairhope, AL 36532
1-800-642-0011

Esslinger & Co.
P.O. Box 64561
St. Paul, MN 55164
(612) 452-7180

Otto Frei-Jules Borel
P.O. Box 796
126 2nd St.
Oakland, CA 94604
(415) 832-0355

Frog Tool Co.
700 W. Jackson Blvd.
Chicago, IL 60606–9990
(312) 648–1270

Heritage Clock Co.
Interstate 85 and Clark Rd.
P.O. Drawer 1577
Lexington, NC 27292
(704) 956–2113

Horton Brasses
Nooks Hill Rd.
P.O. Box 95
Cromwell, CT 06416
(203) 635–4400

M. E. Hurst Assoc.
74 Dynamic Dr., Unit 11
Scarborough, Ontario M1V 3X6
Canada
(416) 293–4497

International Clock Craft, Ltd.
50 Isabel St.
Winnipeg, Manitoba R3A 1E6
(204) 775–8916

Kidder Klock Co.
39 Glen Cameron Rd., Unit 3
Thornhill, Ontario L3T 1P1
Canada
(416) 731–6944

Klockit
P.O. Box 636
Highway H North
Lake Geneva, WI 53147
1-800-556-2548

Kuempel Chime Clock Works
21195 Minnetonka Blvd.
Excelsior, MN 55331
(612) 474–6177

S. La Rose, Inc.
234 Commerce Pl.
Greensboro, NC 27420
(919) 275–0462

Lee Valley Tools
2680 Queensview Dr.
Ottawa, Ontario KBH6
Canada
(613) 596–0350

Mason & Sullivan
210 Wood County Industrial Park
Parkersburg, WV 26101
1-800-535-4482

Midwest Importers
1101 Westport Rd.
Kansas City, MO 64111
(816) 753–5654

Murray Clock Craft Ltd.
510 McNicoll Ave.
Willowdale, Ontario M2H 2E1
Canada
(416) 499–4531

Nautilus Arts and Crafts
6075 Kingston Rd.
West Hill, Ontario M1C 1K5
Canada
(416) 284–1171

Northern Bytes Inc.
45 Uplands
Kitchener, Ontario N9M 4X3
Canada

Reliable Watch Material
1029 Beaver Hall Hill
Montreal, Quebec H2Z 1R9
Canada

Treasure Mart, Ltd.
11171–4 Horseshoe Way
Richmond, British Columbia V7A 4S5
Canada

Tempus fugit *crown-style clock dial. Mason and Sullivan, West Yarmouth, Massachusetts.*

Unicorn Universal Woods, Ltd.
4190 Steeles Ave., W.
Woodbridge, Ontario L4L 3S8
Canada
(416) 851-2308, -8039

Viking Clock Co.
451 Pecan St.
Fairhope, AL 36533
(205) 928-3466

Woodcraft Supply Corp.
210 Wood County Industrial Park
Parkersburg, WV 26101
1-800-535-4482

Wooden Needle
P.O. Box 908
Kamloops, British Columbia
Canada
(604) 554-1624

Yankee Ingenuity
P.O. Box 113
Altus, OK 73522
1-800-537-0464

Glass Supply

See local picture framing, hardware, lumber, or glass outlets for single-strength clear or non-reflective glass. Most of the clock supply companies sell some bevel or straight glass panels in selected sizes. However, the sizes are restricted and selection limited.

Painted or Stained Glass

Check local or area flea markets or hobby and craft retail outlets. If available specimens do not prove satisfactory or cannot be worked into a particular size opening, perhaps a local craftsperson can be located who will produce certain sizes and patterns.

Decals

Check local hardware, paint, or hobby outlets for suitable floral decals. For special decals see major clock supply outlets. Special floral designs and gold "Regulator" decals are available. Automotive stores are a possible source of stripes in assorted colors, and some kits have scrollwork included. These can be applied to glass.

Hardware

Most local lumber, hardware, or hobby outlets carry a full line of suitable cabinet-type hardware. Door catches, pulls, hinges, or glazier's points can be purchased at normal hardware stores. For special items or unusual hardware, such as finials, brackets, or metal feet, see offerings by the major clock supply companies.

FINISHING SUGGESTIONS AND TECHNIQUES

The following techniques have worked very well for me and my woodworking classes and are offered as possible suggestions to complete your clock with a professional finish. If you have a procedure that already works for you, then stay with it. But if you are undecided or want to try something different, test the following techniques and judge their worth for yourself.

Staining

Any good stain will work and darken or color

Battery-operated quartz movement with pendulum. Time Industries Corporation, Sedalia, Colorado.

the wood. My favorites are the oil-based stains. Any national brand stain such as Sears, Watco, Minwax, or Deft will give excellent results. Any hardware, paint, hobby store, or large department store will have oil-based stain available in assorted shades. For best results, apply stain with a paint brush, allow time for penetration, and then wipe the surface with waste cloth. This procedure ensures an even coat, complete coverage, and almost immediate drying to the touch.

The *stain penetration time* needs some explanation. Stain needs time to sink into the wood pores. In softer woods such as pine, butternut, or basswood, the soaking or penetration is almost immediate. After a few moments, the surface is virtually dry and the color is fixed. Hardwoods, such as cherry, maple, or oak, require five to ten minutes more time in order to achieve the proper degree of depth and penetration.

Once the stain is applied and wiped down,

allow the stain coat to dry overnight. Cover this stain coat with several coats of selected finish. Lacquer, varnish, or polyurethane are excellent finishing materials. Follow the directions given on the finish container for best results.

I have obtained very good results with a brushing lacquer product called Deft®. Deft is applied with a brush and dries in one or two hours; therefore, several coats can be applied in one day if desired. (Deft also comes in spray cans.)

Sand the reproduction lightly between coats using 800 (very fine) sandpaper. A white powder may appear, but this is wiped away with a cloth.

It is recommended that four to six coats of Deft be applied in order to obtain the proper field of depth for a professional finish.

When the last coat has been applied and has dried, rub and buff the clock using pumice (or rotten stone) mixed with lemon oil. Rub with the grain only, and wipe the mixture off when a smooth, silky, mellow sheen is achieved. Apply a finishing coat of paste wax as a final protective step, and buff to a satin, velvet hue.

Antiquing

Some reproductions suggest painted colors for a finish. This finish should be toned down from the bright, bold colors achieved directly from the can, into a subtle, slightly aged patina. This process is called antiquing. Paint the clock with a thinned coat of selected paint, preferably a latex-based paint cut with water so that when it is applied, the wood grain will show through. Allow this painted coat to dry, and sand lightly until the desired amount of wood grain is visible.

Cover this painted surface with one coat of Deft or similar finish. When this covering is dry, sand lightly and wipe on a black glaze made up from a mixture of 50 percent flat black paint and 50 percent thinner. Wipe this glaze on with a soft cloth until the desired amount of darkening is achieved. Allow the glaze coat to dry overnight. Apply three to four more coats of Deft or other favorite finish, sanding between every second coat. Finish with pumice and lemon oil followed by a coat of paste wax.

Pennsylvania Dutch–style Painting

Pennsylvania Dutch designs can be applied after first staining or painting the clock reproduction. After this covering has dried, apply one coat of Deft or similar finish. When this coat is dry, paint on the selected Pennsylvania Dutch designs. These designs are painted with bright colors. When the painted designs are dry, wipe on the black glaze previously outlined. Allow the glaze to dry, and then cover with several more coats of Deft or other favorite finish. Rub and buff with pumice and lemon oil, and finish with a coat of paste wax such as Staples Bowling Alley Wax or Butcher's paste wax.